Ella Dietz

The Triumph of Time

Mystical poem

Ella Dietz

The Triumph of Time
Mystical poem

ISBN/EAN: 9783337373450

Printed in Europe, USA, Canada, Australia, Japan

Cover: Foto ©Thomas Meinert / pixelio.de

More available books at **www.hansebooks.com**

𝔐𝔶𝔰𝔱𝔦𝔠𝔞𝔩 ____.

BY

ELLA D___

A SEQUEL TO

TRIUMPH OF LOVE.

LONDON:
ALLEN, 4, AVE MARIA LANE.
MDCCCLXXXIV

All Rights Reserved.

LONDON :
PRINTED BY FARQUHARSON ROBERTS AND PHILLIPS,
13, HUGGIN LANE, E.C.

"That which hath been is now; and that which is to be hath already been; and God requireth that which is past."—ECCLESIASTES iii. 15.

PROLOGUE.

THE GRAVE OF LOVE.

I stand between two lives, a life that's gone,
A life that's dead, yet died to live again;
O unforgotten joys, remembered pain!
Feed all my years with memory alone.
Flow hidden tears, and sorrows deep atone,
For that dear past is dead whom grief hath slain,
Yet green the grave where love so long hath lain,
And roses bloom above one time washed stone.
O days and months and years that are to be,
What gifts bring ye sad fruits of grief and toil?
What treasures from the unrelenting sea?
Heap high your riches, yield the victor spoil.
Lo! at the grave of love on bended knee
I pour as incense all my precious oil.

Part I.

IN ABSENCE.

" Many waters cannot quench love, neither can the floods drown it: If a man would give all the substance of his house for love, it would utterly be contemned."

" Set me as a seal upon thine heart, as a seal upon thine arm : jealousy is cruel as the grave ; the coals thereof are coals of fire, which hath a most vehement flame."

SOLOMON'S SONG viii. 6-7.

SONG.

Dim forms half seen through tears,
Shadows of other years,
Hopes that give way to fears.
    Mists of the morn.

Treasures that seem as lost,
Buds nipped by winter frost,
Count these love's bitter cost.
    O heart forlorn!

Why Did We Part.

Why did we part? I know not how nor why.
My bark has drifted far from love's green shore,
And now the land of light I see no more,
Only a waste of sea, and brooding sky;
The pennon droops that once I proudly bore,
And all the blessed visions seen of yore
Live only as the dead in memory.
When shall the trump sound to awake those dead?
When shall their bodies from the graves arise
And stand confronting us with solemn eyes,
Showing their pierced hands and feet which bled?
Will it then avail our sorrowful surprise?
" These are my little ones," the voice hath said.

When I Am Dead.

When I am dead what man will say
She used to smile in such a way,
Her eyes were dark and strangely bright
As are the solemn stars of night?
What man will say her voice's tone
Was like the far-off winds that moan
Through forest trees? O voice and eyes
That brought me dreams of Paradise!

I think no man, when I am dead,
Will say these things that thou hast said
Unto my living human face,
And all the bloom, and all the grace
Will then be buried out of sight,
Thought of no more, forgotten quite,
As are the flowers of other days,
And songs of birds who sang their praise,
As are the flowers of other springs,
Upon whose grave the wild bird sings.

O flowers and songs of other days!
What sweet new voice will sing your praise?
What choir will celebrate the spring
When love and I went wandering
Between the glades, beneath the trees,
Or by the calm blue summer seas,
And thought no thing beneath the skies
So lovely as each other's eyes?

When we are dead, when both are gone,
Buried in separate graves alone,
Perchance the restless salt sea wave
Will sing its dirge above my grave,
While you, on some far foreign shore,
May hear the distant ocean roar,
And long at last your arms to twine
About this cold dead form of mine.

When we are dead, when both are cold,
When love is as a tale that's told,
Will not our lips so still and mute
Still long for love's untasted fruit?
Though lands and seas hold us apart
Will not my dead heart reach thy heart,
And call to thee from farthest space
Until we both stand face to face?

When we are dead, yea, God doth know
When that shall be, if it were so
This moment now, if thou and I
Lay dead together 'neath this sky,
Could any future to us bring
So sad and desolate a thing
As this sad life? nay, can there be
Such sorrow in eternity?

O long sad days! we need in truth
Some recompense for our lost youth:
By woes forlorn, and sins forborne,
By joys renounced or from us torn,
By thorns that bore no single rose,
By loving hands that dealt us blows;
We pray that when this life shall cease
We then may know eternal peace.

When we are dead, when sea and air
Have claimed the forms that once were fair,
Will joys of Heaven compensate
For two lone hearts left desolate
On earth so long? Will all these years
Of anxious love and burning tears
Be as the water turned to wine,
The best of all that feast divine?

Sea Waves.

The wild waves dash and roar
Along the shingly shore,
Their voice is near, but Oh! I hear
My loved one's voice no more.

The sea-gulls wheel and fly
Against an amber sky,
And so of yore we watched them soar,
Together he and I.

Wild waves along the shore
Roll on and dash and roar
With ceaseless moan since I alone
Recall those days of yore.

Oh! shall we ever stand
By sea or pleasant land
As once we stood and thought it good
Hand closely clasped in hand?

Oh! shall it ever be,
By land or flowing sea,
That he and I beneath the sky
May clasp hands silently?

Though we may never stand
Together on green land,
In Heaven above I'll meet my love
And take him by the hand.

Though it should never be,
Again by land or sea,
In Paradise I'll greet his eyes,
And they shall look on me.

ASPIRATION.

"From me is thy fruit found."—HOSEA xiv. 8.

I am the vine, ye are the branches."—ST. JOHN xv. 5.

My soul must feed on heavenly fruits,
My feet must walk in heavenly ways,
I cannot live by bread alone.
Thy word, O God! my spirit stays,
Remember all my weary days,
Remember, Lord, my parched roots,
Then let Thy will in me be done,
That I may bring forth heavenly fruits.

"Inasmuch as ye did it unto the least of these My little ones, ye did it unto Me."

Unto Thee, my God, unto Thee,
Alas! what have I done?
What angry word not spoken,
What deep made vow not broken.
And now I stand alone,
Filled full of grief and shame,
Self scorn and bitter blame;
Oh! let Thy Holy Name
In me atone.
Though cankering sin doth cling and cleave to me,
Lord set me free!

Unto Thee, my God, unto Thee,
When have I ministered?
When have I given Thee bread?
Has Thy hungry heart been fed
By my thought or deed or word?
Oh! poor and weak am I,
Yet Jesus heed my cry.
Thou wilt not pass me by.
Yea, Thou hast heard.
My broken heart at last I give to Thee.
Christ, set me free!

Sonnet.

"That where I am ye may be also."

That where Thou art Thy chosen ones may be,
Thy chosen ones to sit upon Thy throne,
As Thou hast shared Thy Father's throne alone,
So may we share Thy throne and be with Thee,
With Thee, sweet Lord, throughout eternity;
With Thee who art as God and with Him one,
For where Thou art His will is ever done,
And there all angels praise His unity.
O faithful, holy, wonderful, and true,
Defend me now, let no man take my crown;
Oh! cleanse my life; Yea, cleanse my heart anew;
But bear me up lest in the deeps I drown,
From many called, the chosen are but few,
Who smite the Son must meet the Father's frown

Sweeter than Honey.

Sweeter than honey in the honeycomb
Are Thy sweet words, O Father, unto me,
Like some lost exile seeking after home,
Thus have I sought and found myself in Thee.
Prized above all gold and precious stones
Are Thy commandments written on my heart,
Thy voice is clearer than the dove's low tones,
There is no night nor darkness where Thou art.
Blest are the pure in heart for they shall see
Their God; Oh! rapture to behold His face,
Our blessed Lord who comes to set us free,
And lead His wandering sheep to resting place.
Come quickly, O Lord Jesus! quickly come,
That Thy meek souls of earth may find their home.

Waters in the Desert.

Long time I wandered in a barren land,
My stumbling feet beset by unknown ways,
The scorching sun blinding my weary gaze,
A brazen sky above a waste of sand,
No shelter from the torturing burning rays:
O God! I cried, end now my nights and days,
Smite me with death, yea, strike me where I stand.
And Thou did'st smite as Moses smote the rock,
Not unto death, for forth there gushing flowed
A stream of life, and suddenly there glowed
Bright roses where had been an earthquake's shock,
And grasses green appeared, and cattle lowed,
And by a stream a shepherd fed his flock.

I Gave Thee Jewels.

I gave thee jewels, priceless jewels set
In a crown of gold; I gave thee blooming flowers,
Plucked in an eastern land from sacred bowers,
I gave thee love; that love can'st thou forget?
Can'st thou wipe out the day our spirits met?
Resign the throne and crown that once was ours?
Yield up thy freedom to earth's tyrannous powers?
Obliterate thy love and thy regret?
Yea, thou hast left me; only in my dreams
Do I behold the wonder of thy face,
Across my cloudy sky thy spirit gleams,
A haunting shadow in a lonely place,
Pale as still waters lit by moon's pale beams,
Silent as wings that flying leave no trace.

Nocturne.

Sacred the day we met;
   Sacred the dews that shed
Their drops on the crimson rose,
   In her mossy bed,
When the east was a streak of gold,
   And the west was golden red.

The evening-star trembled for love
   Of the moon's pale light,
Whilst the nightingale in the grove,
   Sang his song to the heart of night.

Still was the air, Oh! still,
   Save the evening breeze
That sighed with a rustling thrill
   Through the forest trees.

Calm was the sky above,
    No sound was heard
Save the throbbing note of love
    From the throbbing bird.

Let those who will forget
    Love's sacred ways;
Mine eyes with tears are wet
    For love's lost days.

Mine eyes with tears are wet,
    My heart is sad,
Let those who will forget
    To make it glad.

The rose is dried and dead,
That once was crimson red,
No sacred dews are shed,
    From out the sky.

Hushed is the nightingale,
Silent his tender wail,
Throughout the darksome vale,
    None hear his cry.

Dark is the face of night,
Thick clouds shut out from sight
The stars, and moon's pale light
    Shut out the sky.

Moaning through quivering trees,
Shudders the sighing breeze,
The shivering waters freeze,
    The streams run dry.

All nature makes her moan,
When love is left alone,
When cold hearts turned to stone,
    Leave love to die.

The Wind Harp.

At night when the stars shine,
My soul is filled with light,
Their bright rays pierce my heart,
I tremble with joy,
Harp-like I sing wild songs,
Glad songs of liberty,
For the cords of my being are strained,
Strained till they vibrate;
And the winds breathe low music through my soul,
I hear the song the wind plays upon my heart:
Its sweetness is ravishing,
I almost faint to hear it;
Between life and death I lie in the land of song.
O death in life thou art sweet!
O life born of death thou art sweeter!

The Song of the Wind.

In the dark night forth going,
    Whither my soul and where?
Whither and where not knowing,
    Forth on the storm-filled air,
Forth on the airy ocean;
    Alone, O my soul! wilt thou dare
To brave the wild wind's dread commotion,
    The darkening gloom of despair?

Forth in the darkness lonely,
    Lone on the open sea,
With thee, O my soul! thee only,
    Sailing the ether free;
While the winds of night are raving,
    And the stars have hid their light,
I with my soul am braving
    The gloom of the deep black night.

Andromeda.

Andromeda upon her lonely rock,
Was not more lone nor more forlorn than I;
Above, the dark face of the barren sky,
And at my feet the cold sea's cruel shock,
The dread sea monster's ravening leering mock;
Why cometh not the saving Perseus? Why
Doomed to a living death do I not die?
Or chained to stone become like stone or stock?
How long, how long swift-footed warrior fair,
Shall woman wait thy coming? When be free?
When thou with thy bright sword shalt cleave the air,
And slay the cruel monster of the sea;   [snare,
Freed from her chains, from rock, from tempter's
She then shall glorify the heavens with thee!

World Weary.

Brother wake and come away,
Where the golden waters gleam ;
Come where flows the sacred stream,
Where the lilies lie asleep,
On the waters cool and deep,
Far away and far away.

Far ; Oh! far our country lies,
'Neath the deep blue tropic skies ;
I can hear the sweet birds call,
I can hear the waters fall ;
Hark ! the sweet birds call us home,
Hark ! they call us ! brother, come !

Brother, wake and take my hand,
I have travelled far alone ;
See behind me white seas moan ;
I have crossed the desert's track
All alone, nor once looked back ;
Left the weary waste of sand
Far behind—A new found land
Full of promise bids us come,
Brother, wake ! and take me home !

The Lost Sheep.

My Father sought my love,
    But night and day
    I turned away;
And ever as He strove,
    In sorrow meek,
    My love to seek,
I ever spurned His love.

I dwelt with mine own pride,
    To Him no gift
    Did I uplift,
Earth's loves I deified;
    I sat in state,
    Queen of my fate,
When lo! one day love died.

Then I cried out in scorn,
    "Is God above
    A God of love?
Why was I ever born?
    Now let Him take
    My soul, and make
Some creature less forlorn."

Then answered He, and spake,
  " I sought thine heart,
  Of mine a part ;
I sought thy thirst to slake,
  Come drink of Me,"
  I said, " be free,
But ye did idols make.

" I give and take away,
  That ye may turn
  To me and burn
With love no man can slay,
  That ye at last
  May hold Me fast,
I give ye power to stray.

" I give ye power to sin,
  If sin ye must,
  Who are as dust,
That I your souls may win ;
  Ye must be free,
  To turn from Me,
As to return within."

But still I strayed away,
 Earth's fruits to eat,
 And called them sweet,
And still forgot to pray;
 My Lord looked down,
 With jealous frown,
My idols turned to clay.

And then I saw my soul,
 Blackened with sin,
 And dark within;
I heard the thunders roll,
 "O God! I cried,
 Would I had died,
Can'st Thou not make me whole?

"At last I come to Thee,
 Oh! let me hear
 Thy voice, nor fear
Thy gracious face to see,
 Unworthy I,
 To live or die,
Unworthy e'en to be.

" Lord, I believe Thy power,
    Thou can'st remake
    My soul and take
Me up at this last hour ;
    Oh ! make me Thine,
    By love Divine,
My strength, my shield, my tower.

" Thy love hath walled me in,
    By night and day
    I cannot stray,
Yea, walled by mine own sin,
    Thus bound to Thee,
    In liberty,
I'm Thine, without, within."

Interlude.

———◆———

THE TENOR VOICE.

Wingèd Sleep.

Lo! in the night with my arms wound around thee,
I carry thee far to some clear limpid stream,
There where my love hath recaptured and bound thee,
I kiss thee at will in thy deep mystic dream.

Child of the lotos, and pearl of the ocean,
Queen of my bosom, and queen of the air,
I call thy deep soul to receive my devotion,
And whisper delight to thy spirit most fair.

Day may divide us, but night-time unites us,
Dreams shall restore us to music and love,
A dream of enchantment that lures and invites us
To groves of sweet spices, the home of the dove.

What though our feet tread the earth on the morrow,
To-night we are wingèd, to-night we are free,
Let me drink deep of joy, forget earth and its sorrow,
And bask in the love-light of Heaven and thee.

We will rest 'neath the palms, we will bathe in clear waters,
Where thy sisters the lilies are waking from sleep,
They will call thee the fairest of all earth's fair daughters,
And amid thy long tresses they'll lovingly creep.

The soft breezes woo us, the birds sing above us,
The waters caress us, the white lilies shine,
All nature rejoices to hold and to love us,
And shares in our mystical rapture divine.

Through the cool shady groves let us wander together,
And eat of the fruit of each blossoming tree,
A garden of spices in balmy spring weather,
Where sweet doves are cooing and calling for thee.

Now the low song of birds my dear love is awaking,
A soft tender kiss on her lips I will press,
And now the bright day her sweet soul is re-taking,
She will wake and remember her lover's caress.

Thine eyes are my starlight, thy face is my moonlight,
Thy hair is my sunlight, thy lips are my morn,
Let me kiss them, night wanes and the day waxes soon bright,
And lo! from my heart a new love lay is born.

Part I.

(CONTINUED.)

Avenged.

Forget me, Oh! forget me; let me be
By thee forgotten, dead and out of sight,
Yea, more than dead, obliterated quite
From out the records of thy memory;
Strew my white ashes to the foaming sea,
Cast them away in darkness of the night;
Let this pale form that once was thy delight,
Be blotted out from earth, from Heaven, from thee.
Then when resolved to dew and fire and air,
Or turned to dust lying beneath thy feet,
When all my dissolution is complete;
Then let some woman rise serenely fair,
Saying with voice unutterably sweet,
Behold in me thy dead love's dead despair.

Relenting.

"Sweetheart," he said; "what sweeter word than this
Can lover call the lady of his love?
O sweet sweetheart!" and therewith fell a kiss
Upon my brow as falls a fluttering dove.
Oh! will that blessed word fall on mine ear
Again from those dear lips? and is it meet
To leave this heart a prey to doubt and fear?
This heart which you beholding called most sweet.
No other eye hath seen its inmost shrine,
No other ear hath heard its inmost voice,
For thee alone it sang its song divine,
And can'st thou now reject thine own heart's choice?
Cast me not from thee on life's bitter sea,
Thou know'st, O love! my Heaven lies hid in thee.

Yearning.

We walk through life o'er steep and stony ways,
We singers who make other lives so sweet,
We gain the heights with torn and bleeding feet,
And hear perchance some far-off word of praise,
Some talk of crowns, faint odours of green bays
Borne on the wind—while voices still repeat
Our songs of early love, we yearn to greet
Some radiant face lost now these many days.
The multitudes may echo what we sing,
Or list with bated breath to thrilling strain,
Born of a soul tortured by lonely pain;
But while we hear the loud applauses ring,
Our hungering hearts would give them all to bring
One vision back, one lost hope to regain.

Light in Darkness.

Where art thou, O my love? where art thou? where?
Will time console me ever for thy loss?
Behold, I bear alone my heavy cross,
And thou alone thy thorny crown doth wear,
Alone? not so, O my beloved! there
Above us stands the One;—our love as dross
Beside His gold doth show, though billows toss
Between us we may walk where faith doth dare.
Our Master leads, we follow on His way,
Follow the self same hand, the tender voice,
Nightly we kneel and to one God we pray,
Daily the gladsome sun doth both rejoice;
He leads us still, earth cannot our hearts sever,
Our God doth guide us now and will for ever.

STRONG AS DEATH.

I loved, God took my love, I did not die,
I love my lost one still, and God knows why;
    O me! the love God gave,
    Must either kill or save,
    'Twill follow to my grave,
      And with me lie.

My star was shining bright, it shines no more,
Quenched is its golden light, dark is my shore,
    I watch for its lost beam,
    When will its radiant gleam
    Light up my darkened dream,
      With light of yore?

My bird that sweetly sang has taken flight,
Its voice now throbs no more through shades of [night;
    I'm suddenly bereaved,
    By hope and love deceived,
    My losses unretrieved,
      Sad is my plight.

Some balmy night my lost bird will return,
Low in the eastern sky my star will burn,
    And o'er my silent grave,
    Where the tall grass will wave,
    The heart I longed to save,
    Will weep and yearn.

Dreams of the Night.

I.

Sweet are my dreams of thee, O love! to-night,
Sweet be thy dreams and peaceful be thy rest,
Upon thy heart may wingëd thoughts alight,
To soothe all troubled yearnings of thy breast;
Oh! hold me fast within thy strong embrace,
Yea, let me nestle deep within thy heart,
There let me find my own abiding place;
My only home on earth is where thou art,
Thy heart my Heaven, my home and my domain,
Cast me not forth in outer night to dwell,
Lift me to thee and let me ever reign
Within thy soul, as by some mystic spell
I draw thee to me, nearer ever nearer,
Till soul and flesh and mind are even as one,
And time will only serve to make us dearer
Each to the other until work be done,
Then o'er our hearts eternal rest shall steal,
And waiting death immortal life reveal.

Joy in Sorrow.

Another year has come and gone,
   Another autumn flown,
Another winter coming on,
   Still finds me here alone,
And many a hope that once was mine,
I now with summer joys resign.

The gay green fields I used to tread,
   Are white with covering snow,
And many a pale sweet blossom's dead,
   That never more shall blow,
And where the flowers lie buried deep,
My hopes and dreams are wrapt in sleep.

We know the glowing springtide sun,
   Will wake to life new flowers,
And after winter's race is run,
   New summers shall be ours,
But what can wake to life again,
The roses spoiled by autumn's rain?

O golden mists upon the hills!
    O vanished land of dreams!
E'en now your memory stirs and thrills
    My heart's fast frozen streams,
Methinks some glad warm springlike day,
Might melt these icy chains away.

Yea, flowers may die and bright hopes fade,
    But let the glad sun glow,
And soon on field and hill and glade,
    A thousand blossoms blow,
And joyful nature doth repeat
Each bygone form and odour sweet.

And so, methinks, if thou should'st come,
    In some glad far-off spring,
And call my heart again thy home,
    And bid it gaily sing,
That tender hopes long, long concealed,
Would bloom like flowers by spring revealed.

And in the blossoms we might see,
    The faces of our dead,
And find the glad reality,
    Sweeter than dreams once fled,
And weep no more o'er our sad past,
Since time restores all joys at last.

Twilight Mists.

Twilight has fallen on the sea,
A winter twilight cold and gray,
And once again I wend my way
Along the rough and shingly shore;
The restless waters hoarsely roar,
Their moaning voices seem to say,
" Where are the days ye loved of yore ? "

Twilight has fallen on the sea,
And through the lowering clouds of night
Shine long pale streaks of fading light,
And far across the water gleams
Red light in intermittent streams,
To warn or cheer the mariner's sight,
As of his longed-for home he dreams.

Twilight has fallen on the sea,
And on the level stretch of land,
On sea and shore and barren strand;
And I alone the one dark spot,
Against the waste of gray a blot;
Would the cold waves might cover me,
Twilight has fallen on the sea !

Dreams of the Night.

Last night I saw my love, I dreamed
    He smiled upon me through his tears;
How sweet and true the vision seemed,
    My love whom I've not seen for years.
He smiled upon me through his tears,
    And gave to me a golden ring;
My love whom I've not seen for years,
    My heart for joy began to sing.

He spoke some low and loving words,
    I laughed for joy and laughed again;
Methought I heard the voice of birds,
    And pattering of gentle rain.
The soft and gently dripping rain,
    That snugly housed one likes to hear;
I laughed for peace and laughed again,
    And knew no care nor any fear.

O haunting vision of the night!
    Come true, O dream! by night or day,
In early dawn or dim twilight,
    In gladsome spring or autumn gray;
Whene'er it be I'll bless the day
    That brings my love in rain or shine;
In golden dawn or twilight gray,
    I'll bless the hour that makes him mine!

Hymn of Praise.

"Praise the Lord, O my soul, and forget not all His benefits:"
"We praise Thee, O God, we acknowledge Thee to be the Lord."

Father of all, who hast given the dawn and the dew,
The night and the stars, which are but as shadows of Thee;
We bathe in Thy light, and our souls are reborn and made new,
We kneel in Thy sight, and arise with our pinions set free.

Thou hast given us songs for our joy, and laments for our sorrow,
Thou hast given the rushing of rivers, the murmurs of seas,
Thou hast given us dreams of the night, and new life on the morrow,
Thy hand is the hand that hath made and hath given us these.

We praise Thee, O Lord, for all our ineffable pleasures,
The light of Thy face, Thy law and Thy love unto men;
Deep cries unto deep, and earth with her bright hidden treasures,
Doth glorify Thee, and re-echoes Thy praises again.

We praise Thee on mountains and hills, on Thy
    high Holy places,
The tall cedar trees sing Thy praises, the pines and
    the firs,
All earth in her beauty but mirrors Thy love, and
    Thy graces
Are seen in each flower of the field which the light
    zephyr stirs.

Each June brings its roses, the shadows of roses
    supernal,
Each autumn its vintage, its harvest of fruits and
    of flowers,
And these blessings of earth are but types of the
    blessings eternal,
Eternal as time with its pageant of days and of
    hours.

Oh! hide not Thy face nor Thy light, though in
    darkness Thou shinest,
We know and acknowledge that Thou art our Lord
    and our God,
Without Thee all pleasures are dead, and joys e'en
    the divinest
Become as the dust of the earth which our feet
    have downtrod.

Pre-Vision.

When the first signs of morning streak
  The eastern sky, will I awake,
And straightway will my loved one seek,
  While yet the day begins to break.

Upon his brow cool blossoms lay,
  Fresh gathered from the dewy green;
And bid the zephyrs lightly play,
  Nor wake him from his dream serene.

While the lark circling sings on high,
  And pierces heaven with her notes,
Which falling from the far-off sky
  Like echoing songs from angel throats

Do intersperse his slumbers sweet,
  Bringing bright visions of delight,
And while those swelling notes retreat,
  The day apace comes conquering night.

Then will my lover lift his eyes,
  And wondering see me where I stand,—
Filled with a joyful glad surprise,
  Will reach to me his willing hand.

And there in that sweet dewy morn,
   The earth filled full of tenderness,
In that sweet day but newly born,
   We two will then our love confess.

We two will then redeem the past,
   Fulfil the promise of lost days,
The spoken word restored at last,
   After long wanderings, long delays.

God is not mocked, the miser's gold
   Is scattered; and the fallen tree
Lies where it fell, and manifold
   Bright gifts thy Lord requires of thee.

The blooming flower, the hidden gem,
   The dewy morn, the sun's bright ray,
Set thou within His diadem,
   And crown Him on His Sabbath day.

WRESTLING.

My God, I love Thee, make me pure
    And sweet and blessed in his eyes;
Without Thy grace could I endure
    The mysteries of Paradise?
Fill Thou my heart with holy fire,
As his is filled with deep desire.

I cling to Thee, Thou Holy One,
    I needs must wrestle and prevail;
Oh! let Thy will in me be done,
    Let not Thy spoken promise fail;
Though sight be dull and clouds be dense,
I feel Thy love's omnipotence.

Clothe me with garments pure and white,
    And make me glorious within;
Living for ever in Thy sight,
    Purged shall I be from secret sin,
And gazing evermore on Thee,
Changed to Thy likeness I shall be.

Tyre.

Ezekiel xxviii.

Purple Tyre, purple Tyre,
    Thou city of the sea,
With many a gleaming golden spire,
    And blazoned canopy;
Thy Prince did walk the stones of fire,
    Ere thou began'st to be.

Between the holy cherubim,
    Thy diadem was set;
Why are thy glories now grown dim,
    Thy name a vain regret?
Why dost thou no more honour him,
    Thy King? dost thou forget?

The jasper and the onyx stone
    Were set within their place;
Thy Prince did trust their power alone,
    Nor sought the Holy Face,
And nevermore can'st thou atone,
    Since thou hast lost His grace.

With precious gems for covering,
   Thy beauty was complete;
The dancers with their pipes did sing
   Down every golden street;
And ships from far-off lands did bring
   Rich stuffs and spices sweet.

The sardius and the topaz gem,
   The sapphire and the gold,
That shone within thy diadem,
   Have made thy heart grow bold;
Thy pride has grown because of them,
   And rich things bought and sold.

Thy traffic and thy merchandise
   Have made thy heart to sin:
Because thou said'st, "I am all wise,
   And glorious within,"
Behold, in dust thy beauty lies,
   Destruction doth begin.

And I will cast thee to the ground,
   That kings may thee behold,
And thou shalt nevermore be found
   Upon thy throne of gold;
And sad thy murmured name shall sound,
   So glorious of old.

Because thy heart once lifted up
    Unto the Throne of God,
Where thou did'st drink the Holy cup
    In pride those heights hath trod,
I cast thee down and thou must sup
    Beneath the scourging rod.

And fire shall in the midst of thee
    Devouring horror spread,
And all the purple flowing sea
    Shall with thy flames be red;
Thou who wert beautiful and free
    Art numbered with the dead.

WEARY.

No rest, no rest, my heart must sing,
    Must sing till it be dead;
Then let the winds of autumn fling
    The rose-leaves o'er my head,
And let white storms of winter bring
    A covering for my bed.

No rest, no rest, for those who toil,
    Must toil till work be done,
Robbing the spoiler of his spoil
    Till victory be won,
With plodding patient care and moil,
    Till the long race be run.

No rest, no rest while life shall last,
    From singing or from pain;
When, when shall all my toil be past,
    When shall my loss be gain?
Will some dim future far and vast
    Unite us severed twain?

Then might I rest as one who sleeps
    And dreams of Paradise,
Feeling above great azure deeps,
    And holy starry eyes
Of One who sacred vigil keeps
    Within the sacred skies.

The Comforter.

Abide with me thou Holy Dove,
    Abide with me, abide with me,
Transform my being by Thy love,
    And set me free! and set me free!

Thy tender voice I long to hear
    That shall me from my sin release;
I wait with trembling joy and fear
    Thy visions of eternal peace.

Abide with me through all my days,
    My will direct, my footsteps guide,
And lead me in Love's righteous ways,
    And from temptation let me hide.

Be Thou a seal upon my heart,
    Let Thy power strengthen and defend,
Till death shall bring me where Thou art,
    And life immortal crown my end.

The Song of the Dove.

Dost thou not hear my singing,
When I my way am winging
    Near and more near,
And to thy lone-heart bringing
    Blessing and cheer?

High up the white clouds float,
Yet hear my piercing note
    Higher than clouds;
Hear how the long notes rise,
And lo! within the skies
    Faces in crowds!

Sweet cherub faces bringing
    Sweet notes to swell the song;
Hear! hear the choral singing,
    Hear! hear the angel throng,
And bright flowers they are flinging,
    To heal the world of wrong.

Bright flowers and songs of glory
    To heal the waiting earth,
To tell the glad old story
    Of the Redeemer's birth,
That through the ages hoary,
    Has saved the world from dearth.

Sing, sing the glad to-morrow
　　Of ages yet to be,
When earth redeemed from sorrow
　　Shall make her children free,
And e'en from time shall borrow,
　　To swell the jubilee.

There shall be sounds of dancing,
　　Instead of silent tears;
There shall be songs entrancing,
　　Dispelling darksome fears;
And eyes with love-light glancing
　　Through all the waiting years.

There shall be holy faces,
　　Watching within the sky,
And joy in heavenly places,
　　And prayers ascending high,
And sweet ethereal graces
　　Beaming from every eye.

There shall be children clinging
　　To the dear Mother's breast,
There shall be angels winging
　　Their way to homes of rest,
And all the glad earth singing
　　Of a Redeemer blest.

THE TRIUMPH OF TIME.

Oh! sweet the infant voices,
   And sweet the songs of praise,
My thankful soul rejoices
   At wisdom's holy days,
When every being's choice is
   To walk in heavenly ways.

When earth has ceased its sighing,
   Being redeemed from sin,
And every heart is crying
   To be made pure within,
And death itself is dying
   That new life may begin.

I bring earth songs of gladness,
   I bring earth songs of peace,
I banish every sadness,
   The captive I release,
I comfort every madness,
   I bid all wars to cease.

I bind the broken-hearted,
   And I restore the slain,
And those long since departed
   I call to life again;
And eyes where tears have started
   I wipe, and heal all pain.

No longer sounds of weeping,
    But sounds of tender mirth,
And, while the dead are sleeping,
    Our joy shall have new birth,
And, with new gladness leaping,
    Shall dance the radiant earth.

Jerusalem our mother,
    Descending from on high,
Shall bring to every brother
    A blessing from the sky;
And each shall see the other
    With love's redeeming eye.

Oh! days of rapturous wonder,
    When every eye shall see;
The veil is rent asunder,
    The people shall be free;
The seven voices thunder
    His Word of Liberty.

Dead Desire.

"Hope deferred maketh the heart sick."—Proverbs.

I would not see thee now, ah, no!
   Nor call the dear past back again,
For how shall summer roses blow
   In chill November's rain?
And how shall hearts that now are cold
Meet as they used to meet of old?

I loved thee, yea, I love thee still,
   But as thou wert, not as thou art;
My dreams of thee must serve to thrill
   The pulses of my heart,
For thou thyself might'st now dispel
The memories I love so well.

I loved thee, and my love was lost,
   A shipwrecked bark on storm-tossed sea;
I ventured all and paid the cost;
   But let no wild tides bring to me
The drift and wreck of that rude gale,
The shivered mast and wind-torn sail.

Enough! One year of love was mine,
   One year of joy, oh! more than sweet;
A harvest rich of corn and wine,
   Gathered with sound of dancing feet;
But now that those dear days are fled,
Let the dead year bury its dead.

Part II.

THE WORD RESTORED.

"Come now, and let us reason together, saith the Lord: though your sins be as scarlet, they shall be as white as snow; though they be red like crimson. they shall be as wool."—ISAIAH i. 18.

"As far as the east is from the west, so far hath He removed our transgressions from us."—PSALM ciii. 12.

"These are they which came out of great tribulation, and have washed their robes and made them white in the blood of the Lamb."—REV. xii. 14.

"I am the resurrection, and the life : he that believeth in me, though he were dead yet shall he live : and whosoever liveth and believeth in Me shall never die."—
ST. JOHN xi. 25-26.

"So shall my word be that goeth forth out of my mouth ; it shall not return unto me void, but it shall accomplish that which I please, and it shall prosper in the thing whereto I sent it."—ISAIAH lv. 11.

"As one whom his mother comforteth, so will I comfort you ; and ye shall be comforted in Jerusalem."—
ISAIAH lxvi. 13.

Hymeneal Hymn.

My lover is strong and terrible,
Like the whirlwind in the valleys,
Like the storm-cloud on the mountain;
He speaks and my soul trembles,
My soul trembles with fear and joy.

Like the pine trees my soul quivers,
Like the pine trees, when, swiftly rushing,
Shaking their lofty branches,
The wind cometh from afar.

Sing on the high mountains,
Sing in the low valleys,
Sing young men and maidens,
Sing, sing for love and joy.

He whom my soul loveth,
He, my own soul's belovèd,
He, chosen out of all men,
He calls me by my name.

He leads me in the valleys,
He bears me up the mountains,
He lifts me where the eagles
Build nests and rear their young.

High up in rocky places,
Low down among the valleys,
Where tender flowers are springing,
Where gentle breezes blow.

He, with strong arms around me,
Guides me in dangerous passes,
Cheers me with words of comfort,
Points to the polar star.

Stars in his eyes reflected,
Brighter than steel his glances,
Swifter than barbèd arrows
Piercing with light my heart.

Oh, sing for he has called me,
Called me to be his helpmeet,
Called me to walk beside him
Through life and unto death.

Called me to scale the mountains,
Called me to dwell in valleys,
Called me to live in freedom
Under God's holy sky.

Darker than night, his locks are
Black as the raven's plumage,
Like clouds of night his tresses,
Like stars of night his eyes.

By rocks and rushing rivers,
Green glades and gladsome places,
There will he gently lead me,
There will he make me rest.

Fair is his face as summer,
Tender as early blossoms,
Fruit trees with blossoms laden,
Like his most tender smiles.

O young men and maidens!
Sing when my lover passes,
Sing him glad songs of welcome,
Songs of the morning star.

Sing, birds, when day is dawning,
Low songs of coming summer,
Sweet songs of glowing sunlight,
Songs of the golden sun.

Flowers in the vales upspringing,
Vines twining into garlands,
Low flowers among the hedges,
Bloom for my love is near.

Wild flowers among the woodlands,
Gay flowers in sunny gardens,
Hillsides and purple mountains,
Bloom for my love has come.

Break, break the bonds of winter,
Trees shake your greenest garments,
High up in slender branches,
Woo, birds, and build your nests.

He whom my soul loveth,
He, my own soul's belovèd,
He, chosen out of all men,
Calls me to be his own.

Calls me to share his splendor,
Calls me to be his helpmeet,
Calls me to walk beside him,
Under God's holy sky.

Gems in the hidden places,
These are my lover's treasures,
Gold from the rocks and mountains,
Gold from the secret mine.

Bright gems of radiant colour,
Sparkling with limpid beauty,
Gleaming on neck and bosom,
Clasping the slender arm.

Pearls in my waving tresses,
Strung pearls, like snow on silver,
Pearls like the moon in waters,
These will my lover bring.

Turquoise like skies at even,
Blue as the flowers of brooklets,
Blue as the eyes of maidens,
This will my lover give.

I, clad in golden raiment,
Wearing his gems upon me,
Clothed thus with love and gladness,
Gladly will shout and sing.

So with my train of maidens
I will go forth to meet him,
Treading the earth's green carpet
Under my happy feet.

Walking in joyous measure,
Singing with happy voices,
We will go forth to greet him,
Him whom my soul doth love.

Eyes as the stars of heaven,
Hair like the night for blackness,
Fair face like dawning summer,
Brow like the brow of kings.

Strong is my love, and tender,
Brighter than steel his glances,
Swifter than barbèd arrows
Piercing with light my heart.

Lo! how my soul doth tremble
Like trees when winds are rushing,
Yea, all my soul doth quiver
Like leaves when winds do blow.

Come, love, into thy garden,
Come where the spice is growing,
Come where my soul awaits thee,
Come where my glad heart sings.

Strong are his arms to hold me,
Strong are his hands to lead me,
Strong is his heart to love me,
Strong are his eagle wings.

High on the mountain summit,
Cold in the heat of summer,
Breathing the clearest ether,
There will we happy dwell.

Low in the greenest valleys,
Warm in the cold of winter,
Cheered by the golden sunlight,
There will we happy dream.

There, with my love beside me,
Lulled by the voice of waters,
Soothed by their distant murmur,
There may we happy sleep.

Rest when the day is over,
Rest when the night is coming,
Rest while the stars are shining,
Clothed with night's silent peace.

Souls sunk in restful slumber,
Bathed with the dews of heaven,
Watched by the starry clusters,
Covered with brooding night.

Chorus.

Blessed be the earth beneath them,
Blessed be the air around them,
Blessed be the sky above them,
Blessed be their holy sleep.

Recompense.

When, after many weary days
   At length I see my loved one's face,
   The goal of life's long weary race,
That joyful moment me repays
For all my hours of tedious toil
   And banishment from his dear sight;
   My woes are then forgotten quite,
Or only serve but as a foil
   To make the present joy more deep,
   As when one sinks in blissful sleep
After a day of rude turmoil.

My woes are past, my griefs are done
   When I can gaze on those dear eyes,
   Whose joyful glance of sweet surprise
Tells me at last my goal is won,
   And, oh, the sense of peaceful rest
   When hand within strong hand is pressed,
Fatigue and weariness are gone,
   Both vanished like a baneful dream,
   And blessèd joy now reigns supreme,
A sceptred queen upon love's throne.

His coming brings me balm and peace,
   My spirit hope and strength regains
   Like parchèd flowers in summer rains ;
His tender words make discords cease;
E'en though we part, thy soul abides
   To soothe and cheer my loneliness ;
   This is my life and my redress,
The thought in which my heart confides,
   That though our lives may lie apart,
   Yet heart must ever beat with heart.

The Land of Silence.

Under green trees, 'mid tender flowers,
   My love would have me dwell,
Where leafy boughs entwine in bowers ;
   A land that I love well,
A land of cool refreshing shade
With far-off glimpse of sunlit glade ;

And where hushed silence, calm and deep,
   Is felt and almost heard,
Till one awakes as if from sleep,
   At sound of far-off bird
Low calling to her distant mate,
Who answering sings " I come love, wait !

So in that hushed and silent land,
    The land of mystic dreams,
I, like a shadow, silent stand
    Where glinting sunlight streams,
And, half awake and half asleep,
My heart doth its long vigil keep.

Only the cry of that lone bird,
    That tender, yearning cry,
Breaking the silence almost heard,
    Waking its mate's reply,
Seems like the call of my lone heart,
And at the sound the tear-drops start;

The tear-drops start and fall from eyes
    Long, long unused to tears,
And tender sobs and broken sighs,
    And passionate hopes and fears,
With dreams of love long laid to rest,
Awake within my yearning breast,

The bird sings loud, it throbs and trills
    "Oh, fly my love to me,"
That pleading note my being thrills,
    "My love, I fly to thee."
The answering bird now loudly sings,
And speeds his way with eager wings.

Awake ! O dreaming heart, awake !
    Lift up thy voice in song
With thrilling tones, the silence break
    With echoes deep and long,
Till that lost wandering heart be found,
Sing till the hills and vales resound.

O lonely bird ! O lonely heart !
    O tender, yearning cry !
Two lives that long had lain apart,
    Now brought for ever nigh ;
Two birds asleep upon one nest,
With naught to break the silence blest.

Sonnet.

"Lord, Thou hast been our dwelling place in all generations."—Psalm xc. 1.

O my belovèd, hide and rest in me,
Sleep, my belovèd, pillowed on my breast,
Sleep on the heart that aches to give thee rest,
Lulled by the murmurs of the distant sea,
The low-voiced waves, the wind's wild minstrelsy,—
Lulled deep in sweet repose and slumbers blest,
Of every care and sorrow dispossessed,
On sleep's light wings we sail the ether free,
For so He giveth His belovèd sleep;
The earth forgetting, they ascend on high
And drink pure draughts from fountains clear and deep,
And find their home eternal in the sky,
Where never a weary soul doth mourn or weep,
For He doth wipe the tears from every eye.

"Seek and Ye shall Find."

I followed far my Love to find,
   I waiting, sought his love to win,
"His heart to God I will rebind,"
   I said "Christ, cleanse his sin!"
I hid my pain from day to day,
   Lest he should grieve to see my grief;
I hid my love and strove to pray,
   But prayer brought no relief:
In some lone place I longed to hide,
And could have laid me down and died.

I sang a hundred songs of love,
   Of love on earth and love in heaven,
Songs of the lonely, cooing dove,
   Of the stars and the colours seven;
The rhythmic sounds of waves and seas
   When moonlit waters washed my feet,
The murmurs of the sighing breeze,
   I wove in music wild and sweet;
I sang of love in ages past,
And of dim futures strange and vast.

My loved one listened to my songs,
    His opening heart grew like a rose ;
As nightingale one note prolongs,
    I sang, and sang " O heart unclose,
O crimson petals deep unfold
    Ere heart be dead within my breast,
Ere beating heart be dead and cold,
    Fold it within its place of rest : "
I know not how it came to be,
But oh ! my Love at last loved me.

At last his radiant eyes sought mine,
    Upon my face his kisses fell ;
My heart was gladdened as with wine,
    And joy too deep for tongue to tell :
O joy, so pure ! O joy, so deep !
    It oped the gates of Paradise ;
And hand-in-hand we fell asleep,
    And felt our wingèd spirits rise,—
Far from the earth, in boundless space,
We sought our heavenly dwelling-place.

Though here we two are sundered yet,
    In heaven our waiting spirits meet ;
O golden days ! When I forget
    Your promise of new days more sweet,
Then let my heart forget to sing
    The songs I learned in Paradise,
And let forgetfulness then bring
    The night of death where no suns rise,
And let my name be known no more
When I forget those days of yore.

Part III.

JUDGMENTS.

"The judgments of the Lord are true and righteous altogether."

Follow after Love.

"Draw me, we will run after."

I followed Love one day,
    He flew away;
Now I must flee,
Oh! will Love follow me?

Will he press after with no turning back,
    Along my painful track?
    I followed him footsore
        In days of yore.

I followed him with weary, bleeding feet,
And though the way was long I found it sweet;
Sweet was the service, sweet the toil and pain,—
    I found it gain.

But now another path I tread,
    Yea, I must go,
    Nor whither do I know,
Perchance with tears to eat of bitter bread,
Yea, silently the hidden tears must flow
    Where I am led.

There is no joy for me in that far land,
  Only the rest that comes when work is done,
  And work is weary when one works alone,
Longing to feel the clasp of one strong hand,
  But work is joyful when two work as one.

Will Love go with me to that lonely land?
  Or will he follow where my steps have led?
Will he uphold me when I scarce can stand?
  When faltering lips still pray for daily bread
Will he with blessings fill my feeble hand,
  · In that far land?

    I may not seek Love now,
      Nay, I must flee;
    I followed Love, oh, will Love follow me;
      He will I trow.

Yea, will he follow with no turning back?
  Will he press after in my losing race?
Will he seek me as once I sought his face?
  If Love be with me I shall nothing lack.

If Love be with me, yea, the wilderness
    Shall nevermore be called a desert place ;
    O Love, sweet Love, let me but see thy face !
And hear thy voice filled full of tenderness ;
My waste of sands shall blossom as the rose,
    And as a giant I shall run my race,
Refreshed by streams where living water flows,
    Held fast in Love's deep heart, in his embrace,
Hidden with him secure where no man knows.

THE SACRIFICIAL DOVES. Lev. xiv.

No. I.

Lo ! I am thine ;
Soul linked with soul and heart entwined with
    Dost thou repine   [heart ;
That thou and I must part ?

    Wilt thou withhold thy dove,
        Thyself from God ?
    Or, on the altar lay
        Thy flesh and blood ?

    Twin doves were we,
        Twin doves upon one nest,
    Circling the ether free,
        Or cooing, breast to breast.

But God required a cleansing sacrifice :
    One to be slain,
And one, living, to rise
    Free o'er the plain,
On the incense-laden air ;
    Wilt thou regain
Thy freedom, wilt thou bear
    Upon thy breast
The blood of thy lost mate ?
    Seeking thy lonely nest,
    Wilt thou await
In loneliness and silence, the long night,
Disconsolate and evermore alone ?
O slain and living bird that shalt atone,
O crimson drops clinging to breast snow-white,
That shall avail to heal and cleanse from sin,
O dear blood shed, sprinkled upon his heart,
    Whose life was bound in thine,
    Yea, deep within.
Part of the living sacrifice thou art,
    The sacrifice divine,
Fitted and joined to every human need,
Yea, part of Him whose flesh is bread indeed,
    Whose blood is living wine.

INTERLUDE.

Grieve not though I should die,
    Grieve not for me;
He doeth all things well,
It shall be well with thee.

It shall be well with thee,
Whether I die or live;
He taketh, he can give;
    Grieve not for me.

Whether I stay or go,
    He doeth all things well;
His ways no man can know,
    His wisdom none can tell.

But trust Him, aching heart,
    Thou shalt not grieve;
Trust Him, let doubt depart,
    Trust and believe.

The Sacrificial Doves. Lev. xiv.

No. II.

I bring to thee the scarlet,
The hyssop and the wood
Of cedar, and the living bird,
To sprinkle with the blood
Of that dead bird in sacrifice,
Then let the living bird arise.

Free on the incense-laden air
    The living bird shall fly,
And on his breast that bird shall bear
    The blood, for one must die;
Oh, which shall live and which be slain,
Since life is loss and death is gain?

Yet both are meet for sacrifice,
    And each would gladly die
So that the other might arise
    In freedom to the sky;
Oh! wilt thou, lonely, live for me
When I am slain, my Love, for thee?

Oh ! wilt thou live when I am gone,
   And bear my crimson blood
Upon thy breast, and fly alone
   O'er hill and plain and wood ?
Yea, bear upon thy snowy breast
That crimson sign from east to west.

That sign that dumbly witnesseth
   Of cleansing by the slain,
Of sacrificial life and death,
   Of double loss and gain.
By life and death we shall atone,
   Living or dead we shall be one.

THE TRIUMPH OF TIME.

"Man cannot live by bread alone."

By bread alone we do not live,
    O God, we live in Thee!
Thy Word must strengthening succour give,
    Thy truth must make us free,
Thy love must make our love increase
And guide us in the paths of peace.

We live in Thee, in Thee we hide,
    No human eye can see
That home where our two souls abide
    In mutual ecstasy;
Though rocky places of the earth
Our feet do tread, we know no dearth.

My Love is comely in mine eyes,
    And I am fair in his;
Oh, more than gold his words I prize,
    Than wine his holy kiss;
And we can bear earth's poverty,
So rich in all love's wealth are we.

The stars shine pure with holy light,
    The birds sing sweet and clear,
The flowers are pleasant to our sight,
    All living things are dear,
For thou art with us, blessèd Lord,
And all obey the living Word.

Saved as by Fire.

I burn my ships, I shall return no more
    To that far land of dreams from whence I came,
My lot is cast upon another shore,
    And on my soul is written a new name;
The past is dead, sealed are my silent lips,
They shall cry out no more; I burn my ships
    And all the sea is reddened by the flame.

I burn my ships that bore me o'er deep seas,
    O'er tropic waters sultry in their calm,
I burn my ships that caught the wakening breeze,
    And bore me far away to Isles of Palm;
Lest siren voices lure me to return,
With sacrificial fire my ships I burn,
    And tune my harp to sing King David's Psalm.

I will return no more; be Thou my rock,
    My fortress, my defence, my hiding place,
Secure with Thee I dread no earthquake shock,
    Thou art my light, hide not Thy holy face;
Deep are Thy judgments, yet in my distress
I am borne up in arms of tenderness,
    Like giant refreshed I run anew my race.

Thy hand was heavy on me day and night,
    And parchèd was my land for lack of rain,
I bowed my soul before Thee, in Thy sight
    Acknowledged all my sins and groaned in pain ;
Then Thou forgavest me and raised me up,
And filled again with wine my fallen cup,
    And gave new life for life that had been slain.

Oh ! shall not I now of thy mercy sing ?
    I trust in Thee, O Lord ! Thou art my God,
My spirit I commit to Thee, O King !
    Who hast redeemed me by Thy chastening rod,
Who hast revealed to me Thy Holy Name,
And purged my soul by judgment and by flame,
    And held me in the paths Thy feet have trod.

I will not fear what man can do to me,
    For am I not Thy daughter, O my King?
Yea, Thou canst bind and Thou canst set me free,
    Silent I wait on Thee or joyful sing ;
When Thou dost bid me, lo ! my voice I'll raise
High to the Heavens in songs of gladdening praise,
    Or stand in silence without questioning.

"There was a noise, and behold a shaking, and the bones came together, bone to his bone.

"Come from the four winds, O breath, and breathe upon these slain, that they may live."—EZEKIEL xxxvii. 7 & 9.

    Flesh of thy flesh I am,
        Bone of thy bone,
    Slain with Thee, spotless Lamb,
        Risen as one,
    Wrapped in God's oriflamme,
        His Will be done.

    Yea, let it be to me
        As my God wills;
    Wingèd life let go free,
        His law fulfils;
    Wingèd life bear with Thee,
        Blood that He spills.

    Sundered we cannot be,
        Whom God has set
    Under His canopy,
        Can God forget?
    His Word was our decree,
        In Him we met.

In Him is hid our life,
    In Him our death,
By Him the sacred knife
    Robs us of breath,
Peace ends our mortal strife,
    Hear what He saith.

He whom my spirit leads,
    Is born of God;
He whom the Father feeds,
    Feels not the rod;
He who in anguish bleeds,
    Christ's ways hath trod.

Part of one sacrifice
    Merged in the slain,
Counted as of great price,
    Holy through pain;
His love shall them suffice,
    His strength sustain.

Lo, it shall be to them
    As they desire,
Set in God's diadem,
    Saved as by fire,
Their glory shall not dim,
    Flames shall aspire.

Thou Knowest.

    Be Thou my Judge!
Thou knowest all my sins and all my woes,
    Be Thou my Judge!
Man cannot judge my cause, for no man knows
The long fierce struggle ere sin overcame
E'en for a little time, the judgment flame
That purged from sin, the cries that heavenward rose
From out my stricken heart; shall I disclose
The stains, the scars, the wounds that grief hath made?
Shall I confess, that all may see my shame?
Or wilt Thou hide me by Thy Holy Name
Where none can me molest or make afraid?
Oh, wilt Thou hide me, Father, in Thy breast,
A stricken dove with bruised and broken wing?
The hunters wounded me, I fly to nest,
Heart-sore, heart-weary, with no strength to sing;
A bruisèd reed, O Father, wilt Thou break,
Or wilt Thou save me for Thine own love's sake?
Only to Thee, the miscreant's hope, I cling,
Only to Thee, O Father, can I cry,
Only to Thee, my Saviour, dare I come;
By law's decree I am condemned to die
An outcast, lonely, without friends or home;
What wilt Thou do for me, O sinners' Friend?
Oh! wilt Thou save and clothe me by Thy grace?

Wilt Thou for poverty Thy riches lend?
Wilt Thou shed light from Thy most Holy Face?
Light that shall guide and strengthen and defend?
Lo! I believe, what other hope have I?
Lo! I believe, dejected as I am,
That Thou canst heal and cleanse and purify;
Washed in Thy Blood, O sacrificial Lamb,
I shall be cleansed from every spot and stain,
Made one with Thee, O holiest of the slain,
Enclosed about as with an oriflamme.
Thy love is boundless, yea, it reaches me.
How shall I limit Thy great power to save?
Thy judgments are as deep as the deep sea,
And jealousy as cruel as the grave;
But love cannot be quenched by waters deep,
And though Thy waves of judgment o'er me sweep,
From out the deeps for mercy still I crave.
Have I not seen Thy mercies with mine eyes?
And Thy salvation hath been very near;
And e'en the life mine enemies despise
Hath in Thy sight been precious and most dear;
Yea, Thou hast lifted me when I have lain
Low in the dust and brought me to Thy feet,
And wiped away the memory of my pain,
And fed me with the food that angels eat,
And though the hunters' arrows pierce me still,
Thou wilt not give them, Father, all their will,
Yea, that last deadly shaft Thou wilt restrain.

I have been fair in my beloved one's sight,
Thou madest me as the lily and the rose,
Thou clothed'st me with the splendours of the night,
The moon's soft beams, the silent, sweet repose
That comes with evening's shades ; Thou gav'st me songs
To soothe his soul to slumbers long and deep ;
Thou fill'dst his heart with pity for the wrongs
That made my heart to bleed, mine eyes to weep ;
However dark had been mine outward sin,
Thou madest me, Lord, all glorious within,
The fairest of all women in his eyes ;
How would it be with me should he despise
The soul of her whom Thou hast made his love ;
If my truth shews as web of woven lies,
How will it be with me? how will it prove?
Plead Thou my cause, O God ! my lips are sealed,
The wounds the hunters made, Thy love hath healed ;
And who shall show the grief that Thou would'st hide?
Plead Thou my cause, O God ! between us stand,
Whom Thou hast joined in heart join now in hand ;
Shew me as One who lives in One who died,
Clothe me with Christ's own power of lowliness,
With meekness, love, and all humility ;
Oh ! let my virtues now atone, redress,

That I may dwell in love's security,
Buried my sin and shame, buried my pride;
Yea, if Thou wilt, I shall be fair as bride
Clothed with the goodness of futurity;
Show me to him as one whom love redeemed
And rescued from the pit of lowest hell;
Show me as one whose garment is unseamed,
Whose living faith can future goodness tell;
Show me as one whom Thou hast loved and crowned,
And healed and cleansed and clothed and made more fair
Than in her first estate; low from the ground
Lift me that I may float in radiant air,
Redeemed by judgment, purged by cleansing fire;
Toward Thy mercy-seat the flames aspire
O sacrifice supreme, O holy flame!
Dead, dead, in Him receive the unwritten name,
The name that shall fulfil your heart's desire.

"Make haste, my beloved, and be thou like to a roe or to a young hart upon the mountains of spices."—
                    Solomon's Song viii. 14.

Like an avalanche my love runs fast,
　My soul is borne away,
Secure within his arms at last,
　I know nor night nor day,
Life, death, and time seem whirling past,
　I feel his power to slay.

But firm in life and firm in death
　My lover holds me fast,
The power of his awakening breath
　Upon my soul is cast,
In all he doth, in all he saith.
　I feel some purpose vast.

He thrills me and he conquers me,
　I know that I am his,
Yet, bound in him, I still am free,
　Sealed by his righteous kiss;
O God of our divinity,
　Seal Thou our holy bliss.

Set Thou Thy seal upon our hearts,
    Control, direct, restrain,
God of mysterious counterparts,
    Seal not our hearts in vain,
Protect us from sin's subtle darts,
    Lest we by sin be slain.

Oh! let us, by thy mercy-seat
    Watching the sacrifice,
Thrice Holy Lord, Thy Name repeat,
    Nor turn away our eyes;
Living upon Thy mercies sweet,
    We dwell in Paradise.

We die with Thee, we live in Thee,
    On Thee our eyes are set,
And sanctified eternally,
    In Thee our souls have met;
Rooted in Thee our wills are free,
    Buried our deep regret.

Christian Marriage.

Husband and Wife.

Husband and wife! O holy names
   Delivered as from God,
To banish strife, saved as by flames,
   Smitten beneath the rod;
The voice of God Himself proclaims
   The way that ye have trod.

Saved as by fire and washed from stains,
   Made glorious within,
Knowing the travail and the pains,
   The suffering of sin,
Knowing the sacrificial gains,
   Feeling Christ's life begin.

Part of the Lamb, forever slain,
   Art thou, O man! to be;
And woman cleansed by love's great pain,
   Jerusalem the free,
Made glorious without a stain,
   God's power descend on thee!

Upon her head the crown shall rest,
    Because angelic wings
Encompass her on heavenly quest,
    And her own angel sings,
Leading her on by visions blest,
    And heavenly comfort brings.

The twelve foundation stones are laid—
    Apostles of the Lamb—
And on the pearly gates displayed,
    Lambent as oriflamme,
The many names in one conveyed
    Of Israel's great I AM.

And learning, glory, wealth and power
    The nations bring to Thee,
O Israel's daughter! yea, thy dower
    Shall more than queenly be;
Upon thy neck, as on a tower,
    Hang shields of majesty.

O virgin daughter! bride most fair!
    Thy clothing of wrought gold
Shall thy inherent grace declare,
    And virtues manifold;
Thy raiment, which the virgins wear
    Shall nevermore wax old.

Forsake thy father's house, O queen!
    Forget thy first estate,
And let thy glorious light be seen
    Shining through eastern gate,
Clear as a crystal white and green,
    Where all the virgins wait.

O bridegroom! love thy lowly bride
    As Christ His Church doth love,
One, who for her perfecting died,
    Waits on His throne above
Until your hearts be sanctified,
    His love on earth to prove,

And bride, in thy dear spouse behold
    The Lamb of sacrifice,
As captive thou wert bought and sold
    Till He laid down thy price;
His blood, more precious far than gold,
    For ransom shall suffice.

The law of liberty is thine,
    The crown of Solomon;
Gaze ever on the face divine,
    Rejoice in victory won,
The marriage feast of bread and wine,
    Declares His reign begun.

Rule in our hearts, Immanuel!
   O Child unto us born,
Thy love shall all our discords quell,
   Thy virtues us adorn;
Put forth Thy rod whose dual spell
   Shall bring Thy bridal morn.

MYSTICAL DEATH.

A little while to love,
   A little while to lie
Upon thy breast, then O my dove!
   To lie alone and die.

A little while to smile,
   A little while to sleep
Upon thy breast, a little while
   And then long days to weep.

Look long in loving eyes,
   Caress the flower-like face,
For parting comes, and death's surprise
   Must unlock love's embrace.

The winds the waters move,
   And like the wind's low sigh
Is fleeting life, and O my love!
   Death will not pass us by!

A fluttering of the heart,
   A quivering of the breath,
Then peace serene in every part:
   Belovèd, this is death.

An aching of the heart,
   A long and weary strife,
Swift tears that tell of sudden smart:
   Belovèd, this is life.

I shall not suffer, sweet,
   When body is laid low,
One long straight line from head to feet,
   And shroud as white as snow.

I shall not suffer much
   When tired heart will not beat
But dream of thine awakening touch,
   And all thy kisses sweet.

Pour oil upon my head,
  Anoint me for the grave,
Nor grieve for me when I am dead,
  For God hath power to save.

From death he calls forth life,
  In life he asks for death,
And His the peace, and His the strife,
  The life-blood and the breath.

"The Strange, Sad Charm of Death."

Oh! let me die and go away,
  Away from all my pain,
I cannot rest, I cannot stay,
  I would not live again,
Oh! let me go to heaven above,
Where I may dream of thee, my love!

I'll watch thee, dear, from that far place,
  And if my silent tears
Fall on thy weeping, upturned face,
  Through the sad lonely years
They'll seem to thee like holy balm,
And soothe thy heart to peaceful calm.

There none will blame and none will chide
   Because I love my love,
All other loves must pale beside
   My only one, my dove;
I, hidden there by leafy screen,
May watch afar and love unseen.

There will I watch and wait for thee,
   In hidden, secret bowers,
O'ershadowed by the Living Tree,
   Plucking immortal flowers;
There will my soul its vigil keep
Till we two sink in endless sleep.

A Night of Roses.

A night of roses! all the air was filled
With strange perfume and odours rare and sweet,
When love came dancing with her wingèd feet,
From out thy heart to mine, my being thrilled
With new delight, and every fear was stilled.
O converse low! O lips that meet and meet,
Sweet as the roses blown in love's retreat,
Sprung from the nectar that the gods had spilled
A night of love! A night of pure delight
With music throbbing through the perfumed air,
Roses blood-red, blush-pink, and creamy white,
Sweet fragrant roses blooming everywhere;
Strange flowers revealèd to our inner sight,
Immortal roses for my love to wear!

Song.

Across the sea, across the sea
Thy dove must fly, thy love must flee,
Oh! wilt thou follow, follow me,
   My love, across the sea?

Across the waste, the watery waste,
Thy dove must speed, thy love must haste;
How like salt tears the sea winds taste,
   Blown from the watery waste.

O'er waters wide, o'er waters wide,
Thy dove must flee, thy love must hide;
Where shall her lonely heart abide,
   Across the waters wide?

Oh! for a nest, a little nest,
Where our two lonely hearts might rest,
Builded by Him who buildeth best,
   One peaceful, holy nest.

Oh! for a place, a resting place
Where we might meet, Love, face to face;
Lord, in the fulness of Thy grace,
   Grant us this resting place.

The Wingèd Harp.

My heart a harp is of a thousand strings,
Thy hand the hand that all its music wakes,
Touch but the chords and into song it breaks,
With quivering delight it throbs and sings,
And like a bird mounts up on airy wings,
Vibrating with the joy the song-bird makes
When from his throat the pearly notes he shakes,
And on the air exultant rapture flings.
O living harp that throbs beneath thy hand!
O wingèd heart that sings through joy or pain!
Fly, fly on wings of song to that bright land,
Where hearts that love can nevermore be twain;
Where loving souls like one fair angel stand
Singing one holy song, one heavenly strain.

"He feedeth among the lilies."
"I sleep, but my heart waketh."

Where lilies blow my Love doth feed,
  Where lilies blow and waters break,
Fly, thoughts, to him, on wings of speed,
  Tell him for him my heart doth wake.

I sleep, but oh! my waking heart
  Doth her long patient vigil keep;
When shall day bring me where thou art
  And Love arouse me from my sleep?

Sonnet.

Henceforth I will believe that thou dost love,
Time shall not blot this vision from my sight,
Nor the long toil of day, nor sleep of night,
Nor power of fate, that doth so far remove
Thy life from mine; these things Love's strength shall prove;
And loving hearts do find his service light;
Would we escape it, loved one, if we might?
We serve on earth to meet in Heaven above.
I will believe, though all the world say nay,
Love is no summer flower that blooms to die;
Love is no mortal child that death can slay.
Hidden beyond the reach of every eye
The rose of love doth bloom eternally,
And in its heart the sleeping God doth lie.

Song.

What hast thou given to me that other men might
    not have given?
Lo! thou hast left me free to bow my soul unstained,
    to One in Heaven,
Nor any thought, or word, or deed, of thine
Hath held my soul from worshipping the Divine.

What have I given to thee that other women, too,
    might not have given?
I bowed on bended knee and lifted high my gift to
    One in Heaven.
God took my heart of flame—His love divine
Read, deep within, a name, that name was thine.

Chorus.

Wingèd heart, wingèd lyre,
Filled with love and holy fire,
God shall make thy life aspire,
    God shall make thee free.

" Hope thou in God, for I shall yet praise Him who is the light of my countenance and my God."

Part III.

BUILDING THE HOUSE.

"The desire of wisdom bringeth to a kingdom. Give me wisdom that sitteth by Thy throne and reject me not from among Thy children. And hardly do we guess aright at things that are upon the earth, and with labour do we find the things that are before us: but the things that are in heaven who hath searched out?

Mysteries are revealed unto the meek."

The Name.

Insatiable desire
For that which is forbidden,
Consumes my bones like fire;
The secret which is hidden
Evades the searching cravings of my lust,
And serpent counsel turns my gods to dust.

Seek, and ye shall find;
Knock, it shall be open;
Laws like fetters bind
Love, (O! word unspoken).
That shall fulfil the letter of the law,
And purge all hearts from every stain and flaw.

Wonderful design,
God and Nature blended,
Harmony divine,
All our discords ended.
The ends of the whole earth on him are poured,
Christ Jesus,—name by every soul adored.

Building the House.

"Except the Lord build the house, they labour in vain that build it; except the Lord keep the city the watchman waketh but in vain." PSALMS cxxvii.

O Thou who taught the bee to build her cell,
And planned a nest for every little bird,
Teach me to build a home where love may dwell,
Where ne'er one note of discord may be heard.
Firm on a rock plant my foundations deep,
Then watch me with Thine eye that doth not sleep,
Encamp me round with cloudy tower and sword.

Except the Lord himself do build my house,
My hands may strive and toil yet nothing gain,
Except the Lord the city keep, arouse
The watchman if ye will, lost is your pain;
In vain ye rise so early, sit up late,
In vain do ye the bread of sorrows eat,
Yea, all your watching and your labour vain.

But build the walls of fair Jerusalem,
The Highest shall Himself establish thee,
With polished corner stones and many a gem,
Set in thy walls a shining galaxy.
Yea, lay her stones with colours fair and fine,
There let the sardius gleam, the sapphire shine,
Set in pure gold brought from beyond the sea.

Of cedar beams the Lord my house shall build,
Of well-cut stones fitted without a sound,
The rafters shall be joined by hands well skilled,
And no unwilling workman shall be found
In all the band of goodly companies,
Hewing the stately fir and cedar trees,
With fitting words they pass the tools around.

In olden time when Hiram, King of Tyre,
Sent messengers to David, builders all,
They built King David's house at his desire,
And laid the stones of the foundation wall.
And all the galleries of fir did make,
And David knew that he for Israel's sake
Established was, their King beyond recall.

Then did his loyal heart and soul require
Another house, where ark of God might rest,
To that high dignity he did aspire,
To build a sanctuary pure and blest,
Where Ark of Covenant might find repose,
And from his lips this mighty prayer arose,
To be of God's great holy name possessed.

God heard, and answered David's righteous prayer,
And gave to him a son to live and reign,
And David knew this son should be his heir,
And build the Temple and great wisdom gain;
And that his line should live in Solomon,
That when his days on earth were past and done,
His seed should after him great power attain.

Thus did the Lord King David's prayer fulfil,
He planted wisdom in his flesh and blood,
In Solomon accomplishèd the will
Of David, whose One seed forever stood.
And shall forever stand, we worship now
The King from David's line, with thorns on brow,
The root and offspring of that kingdom good.

From David's line sweet Mary full of grace
Was found, the willing handmaid of the Lord:
She worshipped, kneeling in the very place
Where David prayed God's name might be adored.
O prayer whose power down all the ages came,
'Till lowly Mary heard the wondrous name,
And in her womb conceived the hidden Word.

O prayer whose power is wrestling with the seed
Of David now, Great King descend again,
The Kingdom that is Thine in very deed,
Idolatry hath rent, parted in twain,
Pray that Thy kingdom now may be made one,
Ruled over, governed, by Thy Lord, the Son;
Christ Jesus come and heal a nation's pain.

We pray that outcast sons may be recalled,
Establishèd the wanderers of Thy tribe,
The princes of the people be installed
With priest, and Levite, warrior and scribe.
O Judah! Judah! when thy King was killed
The earth was ransomed by the blood then spilled;
Behold how God returns the Judas bribe.

Oh! build the house again that He may reign,
Triumphant now o'er all the conquered earth;
Gather the fruits of his celestial pain,
With shouts of joy welcome His second birth.
A nation's prayers and cries at length prevail,
Immanuel comes, Hail! Mary, Mother, Hail!
Through Thee we shall again the Son bring forth.

"The City Lieth Four Square."

To enter in at the straight gate,
Many the things we must leave behind,
But do not tarry, Oh! do not wait,
Lest maimed and halt, or weak and blind
We come at last to the closing door
We should have entered long before,
And hear the voice cry out "Too late."

"Run, run my Love, like hart or hind,"
"Yea, come my sister let us flee,"
"Draw me, we run as swift as wind,
The virgins follow after thee."
The Bridegroom cometh he will not wait,
To lead the Bride through the pearly gate,
And those that are ready the way shall find.

Oh! tell me my Love of that Bride most fair:
Her robe is white linen and broidered gold,
Bright jewels gleam in her shining hair,
The gems on her bosom are manifold.
Like a queen she sits in royal state,
The Bridegroom cometh he will not wait,
But the hour of his coming can none declare.

Bright city, fair things shall be found in thee,
Fair to the sight and sweet to the ear,
Sounds of tabrets and minstrelsy,
Voices of maidens in praises clear.
The kingdom is ready for King and Bride,
And happy are they who are found inside :
Be ready, the Bridegroom we soon shall see.

O city of gardens and pearly gates,
Guarded forever by angel wings,
Blest is the being who penetrates,
To the throne where the great white angel sings.
Blessed is he who can pass through fire
Unscathed to the place of his heart's desire,
And receive his crown from the Bride who waits.

Nought that defileth can enter in,
Only the holy can see their Lord,
Purged by deep judgments from stain and sin,
Smitten asunder by two-edged sword.
O vision of beauty beyond compare,
More bright than the sun, than the moon more fair :
The Queen is crowned, let her reign begin.

Interlude.

CONFESSION AND ABSOLUTION.

"By the waters of Babylon we sat down and wept when we remembered Zion."

I.

I have renounced Love's ways,—Oh! not for me
Blooms the red rose, or wakes the poet's lyre,
Nor shall I reach the goal of my desire,
With unquiet soul as restless as the sea,
Whose moon-swayed tides roll on unceasingly,
With ebb and flow that never seems to tire,
Yet have no power to quench Love's quenchless fire,
Nor from my deep despair to set me free.
We met; and Love arose as from the dead,
For memory filled me with the former grace,
I gazed once more on thy love-lighted face,
And thought the lonely years of sorrow fled.
But now alone in this far desert place,
I know our hungering hearts on husks have fed.

II.

O Love, I bartered all, nor counted cost,
I gave my heart as freely as my life,
And would have smiled had you with deadly knife
Pierced that, for then my soul had not been lost,
Nor all my future with mad tumults tossed;
Fed on the bitter fruits of cruel strife,
Hardened by rankling thoughts, with discords rife,
And all its pleasant places marred and crossed.
Your love like sunshine on my cold life fell,
And soon it turned to soft descending rain,
And 'neath thy touch as by enchanter's spell,
My wintry land blossomed with flowers again,—
Then the mad hurricane in one fell hour,
With rudest blast destroyed each tree and flower.

III.

And thus I tread a path of loneliness
'Mid mountain rocks, o'er sandy desert ways.
Through long and lonely nights, through sultry days,
No voices soothe with songs of tenderness,
No hand binds up my wounds,—in my distress
I dare not list to words of cheerful praise,
And conscience on me heavy burdens lays;
My heart is silent and companionless.

The songs of Zion, how shall they be sung
By the sad streams made bitter by our tears?
Shall tones of gladness from dead hearts be wrung?
What shall atone for sweet youth's wasted years?
The cords have snapt that were too tightly strung,
And all my life a ruinous waste appears.

IV.

And yet from that dead waste there may arise
A glad new heaven, a new created earth;
At His command my soul may have new birth,
And upward wing its flight toward bluer skies.
And see with vision's clear far-reaching eyes
Beyond the discord and beyond the dearth
To that bright land of song and purest mirth
Where angels minister, where babes are wise.
At His command the glorious light appeared,
At His command the waters must divide,
Wisdom restrains that foaming rushing tide,
And at His word the hoary hills were reared;
O Holy Name! to every heart endeared,
O Saving Rock where humblest heart may hide.

The Thread Resumed.

Song.

O sweet oblivion, of all things thou art best,
Never to weep again—ever to rest,
Sunk deep within the deep eternal breast.

When Beauty Fades.

"When Thou with rebukes dost chasten man for sin,
Thou makest his beauty to consume like as it were a moth
fretting a garment; every man therefore is but vanity."
Psalm xxxix. 12.

I.

When beauty fades from off the pallid cheek,
When tender eyes with love-light cease to glow,
When sunny hair bleaching with streaks of snow
Veils the sad face, when voice with age grows weak,
Wilt thou love on, fond lover? wilt thou seek
With loyal care for signs of long ago
When at thy coming many a rose did blow,
And joyous radiance did full welcome speak?
Sufficed with hallowed memories of the past
Wilt thou love on love's promise to fulfil?
Or wilt away that dear remembrance cast
Seeking in present joy that past to kill?
Or wilt thou love me only first and last,
Thy fading rose, that holds love's fragrance still?

II.

So I be fair to thee, I care not when
I lose the bloom that other eyes admire;
When I lose grace for thee let kind hands 'tire
Me in my burial-robes and hide me, then
I shall have lived too long in sight of men.
If thy love fickle prove, let me retire
To some dim solitude, and there expire
Alone, forgotten, out of sight and ken.
Tell me what grace in me first won thy heart?
What did'st thou find in me worthy to prize?
Oh! was it not for some immortal part
Rather than for that fair which fades and dies?
Did'st thou not say " I love thee as thou art
And as thou shalt be when the dead shall rise?"

III.

Yea, love me so before my roses fade,
That thou wilt love me even in the grave;
For that unchanging love my heart doth crave;
The thieving hand of time will not be stayed,
And year by year and month by month are paid
The drops of living blood, and none can save
From his great ravage; stealing like a knave
Stalks Death behind, and will not be gainsayed.

But if thou love me they can do no harm,
I laugh at each when sheltered by sure love ;
Time passes swift and brings me no alarm ;
Death nearer stalks, my soul sits free above ;
Thou dost not love me for my passing charm,
But for that grace which shall eternal prove.

WHEN ROSES BLOOM

When roses bloom in Autumn days,
    Sweet with the fragrance of the Spring,
They bring to mind those leafy ways
    Where thou and I went wandering
In early June—the hawthorn sprays
Were thick with flowers, the cuckoo's lays
    We heard and mocked his questioning.

Now far and faint the breezes sigh
    O'er meadow, brook, and lonely lea ;
A hollow echo says " good-bye "
    Like the sad voice of memory,
And at its sound the roses die,
While cold clouds drift across the sky,
    And wintry night descends on me.

The Sacrament.

Both soul and body now to Thee
   I give if Thou wilt take ;
I am not worthy Thine to be,
   But thou can'st worthy make :
Cleanse me, O Lord, by Thy dear blood,
And let Thy body be my food.

How gracious is Thy comforting,
   O Jesus, man and God !
A contrite heart to Thee I bring
   Smitten by chastening rod ;
On the wild waves of passion tossed,
But for Thy love it had been lost.

The Meeting.

I.

After long years of silent gloom we met,
And sleeping Love leaped from his hiding-place
And laughed for joy to see us face to face.
I looked and saw thine eyes with tears were wet,—
O crystal drops ! that sight made me forget
All former woes, yea, for a little space
Grief vanished quite, subdued by tender grace ;
Thy smiles and tears wiped out all past regret.

Healed are the wounds our sudden parting made,
Those blessed tears like balm brought sweet repose,
Love conquering comes and will not be gainsayed,
Where those drops fell blooms now the fadeless rose,
And every lonely yearning prayer we prayed
Is as a flower that in Love's garden grows.

II.

Yea, in Love's sacred and most hidden bower,
Where heart of man doth ever long to rest,
Folded within thy loved one's tender breast,
Blooms sweet for thee the eternal living flower.
The flaming swords are past, our souls have power
To enter, finding there their life's long quest,
Their lonely toil repaid by rapture blest,
Their grief exchanged for joy's most blissful dower.
When years of waiting love are overpast,
When burdens fall away, O glad release!
When folded in thine arms, secure at last,
I hear thy lips whisper the glad word " Peace,"
" Peace, peace, sweetheart, thy lover holds thee fast,"
Then all my yearnings and my tears shall cease.

III.

Though night be dark, the long watch I will keep,
And wait the dawn of that glad perfect day
Which shall for ever chase night's shades away:
My faithful soul doth wake though I do sleep,
My heart shall sing though I do sigh and weep,
And when I almost faint that heart shall pray,
Keeping my wandering steps lest they should stray,
Guiding my soul through mists and shadows deep.
Pray thou for me, yea, let thy prayers ascend
As incense wafted by soft wings on high,
Returning thence to me from the far sky,
As the soft dews of night on flowers descend;
Their holy calm through all my life shall blend,
And on their wings my prayers shall upward fly.

Song.

O my dear soul!
So far away the white seas over,
   Roll billows roll,
Roll to the feet of my waiting lover.
   Blow breezes blow,
Where my mate sits lonely,
   Make him to know,
I love him only!

Fly, birds! fly!
Through wind and storm, for my heart is waiting,
The Spring is nigh,
Green are the woods where the birds are mating.
Bid him to come
Where my heart sits lonely,
Building a home
For him I love only.

— Song.

Where shall my bark drift,
To what far shore?
Where shall my song lift
Pinions once more?
Where shall I sing of thee,
Under what canopy,
By east or western sea,
Songs as of yore?

WITHIN AND WITHOUT.

Here in my little room
Blush roses bloom,
Without the skies are gray and cold and drear,
 Within there is good cheer,
 Banished is gloom.

My heart is like a rose,
Within whose petals glows
A hidden centre, filled with golden fire,
 There sleeps my heart's desire—
 Sleeps till the south wind blows.

It dare not venture forth
Lest cold winds from the north
Blast the young blossoms of the tender vine
 That promise red new wine,
 Wine without wrath.

And so it sleeps and waits
'Till God shall ope the gates
And bid the poet and the prophet sing—
 Sing without questioning
 The song of Fates.

The Star-Fish.

The star-fish by the sea,
  Left stranded by the tide,
Drew pitying tears from thee;
  While I walked by thy side,
    Lonely and desolate,
Had'st thou no word for me?

Had'st thou no word for me,
  Left stranded by love's tide,
By salt and cruel sea,
  That my poor will defied;
    By mocking fate
That gave my heart to thee?

Thou had'st no word for me
  But only silent pride;
The star-fish but for thee
  Unrescued might have died;
    Was it too late
To find his native sea?

I know not but thy tears
    Were shed alone for him—
For him thy pitying fears,
    For him thine eyes grew dim;
      O sad strange heart,
That saw'st not future years.

Thou saw'st not future years,
    , Wherein our love grew dim,
Wherein salt, bitter tears
    Were shed, but not for him;
      We had to part
That day—what hopes—what fears

Filled my poor eyes with tears,
    Filled to the brim;
My heart that yearned with fears
    To know the future grim;
      How loth to start
When the dark path appears.

O little living star!
    Cast far into the tide
By friendly hand so far,
    My heart fell there beside,
      It followed thee,
One hand can make and mar.

It followed thee, O star!
　　Cast to thy native sea;
One hand can make and mar—
　　The hand that set thee free
　　　　Hath tortured me
And set my love afar.

Hath set my love afar,
　　Cast to the cruel sea;
He gave thee life, O star!
　　But he gave death to me;
　　　　I die, sent free
Where naught can make or mar.

SONNET.

Better the silence that has fallen between
Our aching hearts than loud laments of pain,
Better our tears should fall like summer rain
Than that fierce heat should parch the tender green.
Silence and tears for each, though no more seen
The love-lit eyes—nor voices heard again,
Yet will we bear this fate and not complain
Knowing our spirits meet 'mid airs serene.
A day shall dawn of full and perfect rest,
A night of stars and calm expanding seas
Shall soon descend: the islands of the blest
Await us; while we steer with wakening breeze
Our little bark o'er the deep water's breast,
We hear afar angelic harmonies.

The Hidden Bower.

I may not see thy face,
   I may not touch thy hand,
I may not hear thy voice call
   Across the silent strand;
Thy voice so sweet to hear,
   Thy face so sweet to see,
Thy hand that held my wayward hand
   So firm yet tenderly.
While every bird of Spring
   May call unto its mate,
Our hearts must lonely sing,
   Our hearts must lonely wait.

   Our Spring is gone,
   And Summer time
   Will soon be past;
   Our youth's glad prime
Is fading, while on lonely lea
The Autumn winds blow silently.
And sad, cold Winter steals apace,
And yet I may not see thy face.

So long it seems—the years gone by,
    We met and loved so long ago,
We met, we loved, we know not why,
    O God! and shall we ever know?
So love we still, nor can forget
That day we met, that day we met.

Yet thou art ever near me
    Though ever far away;
I never bow on bended knee
    But for thy soul I pray;
I never sit and watch the sky
    Or distant silent sea,
But that I feel thy spirit nigh,
    And know the ecstacy
Of two communing souls in one,
Adoring as before the Throne.

God gave the love I feel for thee,
    God made that love endure;
I may not from its presence flee,
    It holds my heart secure,
I seek it not, it flies to me
As birds fly homeward from the sea.

It dwells so deep within my heart,
    Far from the world's rude gaze,
None guess how much I live apart,
    Alone to tread Love's ways,
And build a queenly pleasure house
Where dwells my love, my lord, my spouse,
    Whose lightest word is praise.

None see my garden where the rose
    And tender lily wait,
Only my own belovèd knows
    That hidden, secret gate,
And none can pass the flaming sword
Except my love, my heart's one lord;
    He will not tarry late.

The roses red are blowing
    'Mid lilies pure and white,
The fountains clear are flowing,
    And all for his delight;
Spice odours float upon the breeze,
Doves coo in the pomegranate trees;
    And fragrant is the night.

If my love sleep, O daughters!
   Ye may not rouse him yet,
The voice of many waters,
   Cannot make him forget;
For Oh! his love is strong as death,
Born of the fire and living breath,
   And in God's signet set.

Reflected in clear waters,
   We see the starry skies,
Thus his sweet face, O daughters!
   Within my bosom lies;
And though I made my bed in hell,
Far from my love I could not dwell,
   Nor hide from his clear eyes.

God's word alone can sunder,
   God's word alone can seal,
The lightning and the thunder
   His unity reveal;
How blest are they who trusting stand,
Hid in the hollow of His hand,
   And to His love appeal.

How blest are they who slumber,
   As His belovèd sleep,
Who shall be of the number,
   Of His own chosen sheep,
Who know and love the Shepherd's voice,
And when they hear His word, rejoice,
   And His commandments keep.

Thou art as my own brother,
   Nurtured at wisdom's breast;
Born of the self-same mother,
   Within her heart we rest;
Eat of her bread and drink her wine,
O heavenly food! O cup divine!
   End of my life's long quest.

> "Stay me with flagons, comfort me with apples, for I am sick of love."—SONG OF SOLOMON.

Sometimes I almost faint to think
    Of thee and thy sweet face,
My pulses fail, I long to sink
    Deep, deep in thy embrace;
The clear pure colour of thy cheek
    Brings such delight I cannot speak
When dreams reveal thy face.

Sometimes my heart stands dumb and still,
    Thy lips like scarlet thread
O'ercome me with a sudden thrill
    'Till life seems almost fled;
Thy tender beauty passing fair
    So fills my heart with rapture rare,
The earth no more I tread.

I faint for love—I die for love,
    Ah! comfort me my own,
I cannot wear the crown thereof,
    Nor bear its weight alone;
This sudden bliss, this joy intense
    Exalts with rapture every sense
To heights supreme, unknown.

Sustain with me this shaft of light,
   This sudden shower of gold,
Enclose me with thy pinions bright
   Of colours manifold.
Then let us float on silent wings
   To where the great white angel sings
The songs we knew of old.

Autumn Song.

Were I a lady fair—
   Loving dainty pleasure,
   Soft ease and gentle leisure,
With rosebuds in my hair—
   We'd tread a stately measure
Perchance, and you might wear
   My favour as a treasure.

Were you a knight of old,
   We then might love discreetly;
   Tuning our voices sweetly,
With eyes not overbold;
   Yet knowing Love completely,
And his ways manifold,
   We'd follow him so fleetly.

The world has grown unkind,
   I think, since we are chidden
   For loving thus unbidden;
Poor Love is left behind,
   Or in some corner hidden
Away from this rude wind—
   Or has he grown bedridden?

Yet leave him not alone,
   We may not love so brightly,
   So graciously and lightly,
As in the days long gone,
   When men were brave and knightly,
When gallant deeds were done,
   And love vows kept most rightly.

We love now while we sigh,
   "The days are growing colder,
   Our youth is waxing older;
The last pale roses die,
   The Autumn rains will moulder
The blossoms where they lie—
   Yet Love grows never bolder.

" Why did we meet so late—
    We love and cannot sever
    The link that binds us ever—
Ah! who can change his fate?
    We loved once and forever,
We cannot choose but wait,
    Though life unite us never.

" Our love can never fade,
    However ill we use it,
    Reject it or abuse it;
It will <u>not</u> be gainsayed
    'Twere folly to refuse it;
Since it cannot be stayed
    'Twere better far to choose it.

" Grave knight and gentle dame,
    With silver in our tresses;
    (The autumn twilight presses
Where erst the morning came)
    With stately slow addresses,
We call our Love by name—
    Our words seem like caresses.

"The joys of buried spring,
   And years of love are lying,
   Where that pale rose is dying;
The songs we could not sing
   For tears are upward flying
Like birds on merry wing;
   Hills echo in replying.

"O days and years once lost!
   O load of weary trouble!
   Love shall requite us double,
And pay us all ye cost;
   Our grief be as a bubble,
Blown off and gaily toss'd;
   Our sorrows burned as stubble.

In youth love glows like wine,
   We kept our love in tether,
   Ah, love! I wonder whether
We'll taste that draught divine;
   In warm or frosty weather,
I'll care not nor repine,
   So we but drink together."

Song.

Yea, those who tread the desert's track,
    Obedient to his word,
Shall no refreshing comfort lack,
    Nor no defending sword.

At Communion.

Dost Thou not know? Thine eye can read and see,
Thou who hast compassed grief upon the Tree,
Sounding the heights and depths of human woe,
Can my heart feel a pang Thou dost not know?

Dost Thou not care? Thy heart can probe and feel,
Yea, every smile that fain would tears conceal
Reveals my grief to Thee; no bird of air
Can fall unmarked by Thee; dost Thou not care?

Lord of the least of these, or great or small,
Who numberest hairs, markest the sparrow's fall,
My wine is drunk, yea, even to the lees,
My bark is tossing on tempestuous seas.

There is no wine, yet Master by Thy will
The waters turned; and by Thy "Peace be still,"
The tempest slept; Oh! calm this life of mine,
And give me now to drink Thy draught divine.

SONNETS.

I.

I will be calm, I will not speak nor sigh;
I will be brave and hide my deep unrest,
I will be true, and fold within my breast
Each treasured word of Thine, nor make reply
Should the unloving eyes now ask me why
I cease pursuing their too worldly quest,
And treat their vanities as meet for jest;
One who has lived and loved may calmly die.
What can life give more sweet than early love?
Than flowers of May? than nights of balmy June?
Than days when each bird cooed and wooed in tune
From soaring lark to the full-throated dove?
Should death come now to bear our souls above,
We could not say " Alas! he comes too soon."

II.

Too soon ? ah ! no, since led by Love's own hand,
We followed him obedient to his mood ;
For us the tree of evil and of good
Ripened its fruit, untouched in that fair land
Where Love doth dwell,—there by spice odours fanned,
Another tree put forth its living food,
While on the topmost bough the Dove did brood,
And Cherubim with flaming sword did stand.
Deep, deep we sank to rest in long embrace :
Death cannot vanquish now, nor life destroy
The memory of that eternal joy ;
The veil was rent, we saw Love face to face,
And knew his rapture without sin's alloy,
And Paradise became our dwelling place.

Willow Song.

Death is coming, coming late or soon,
No more golden sun, no more silver moon,
No more roses blowing in long days of June,
Death is coming, coming late or soon.

Death is coming, coming soon or late,
Love the laggard lingers, will death wait?
    Love the tardy comer,
    Loiters through the summer,
Whiles that Death is knocking at the gate.

    Oh! good-bye faint-hearted,
      I must flee,
    When I am departed,
      Come and see;
    With thy rose wreaths wind me,
    With thy fetters bind me,
    When that thou shalt find me,
      Flown and free!

Song.

I have an armèd knight,
   Unseen who fights for me,
Moonbeams are not so bright
   As his white panoply;
When shocks his blazing spear,
Falsehood shall disappear;
Before his beaming eye
Cowards must fly!

SONG.

A bonnie bird came flying, swift flying from the west,
He sang so sweetly to my aching heart,
"Poor heart and art thou waiting for the one thou lovest best,
Waiting to meet no more to part?"

A silver cloud came sailing high up in bluest air,
And tenderly it wept to see mine eyes,
For I said, "O cloud I'm longing to be with thee up there,
And seek my own dear true love in the skies."

But the bonnie bird went flying far over summer seas,
And the silver cloud has turned to autumn rain,
And alone beside my hearthstone I hear the sighing breeze,
And my heart is dumb and still with lonely pain.

The Angel of our Love.

In wind and rain, through sleet and snow,
Love follows me where'er I go,
When skies are clear the golden air
Thrills with his presence everywhere;
When skies are dark and overcast
Safe in his arms he holds me fast.

Where'er I go Love follows me,
Nor from his presence could I flee;
His eyes regard me calm and still,
My pleasure is to do their will,
My rapture is to read his face,
And mirror in my heart his grace.

Lord of my life, he reigns supreme,
O'er every thought, desire, or dream,
O'er mind and soul, or heart and sense,
Love reigns with full omnipotence;
My all to him I gladly yield,
Lord of my life, my heart's bright shield.

The Dual Vision.

I.

Upon the mount, O Lord! I saw Thy face,
Transfigured with exceeding glory round,
With rapturous awe I fell upon the ground
Crying " 'Tis good to be here in this place
Tasting celestial joys filled full of grace."
My spirit compassed Heaven as at a bound,
And heard the praises from the deeps resound,
Nor could I back to earth my steps retrace.
I slept and woke to find no longer there
The glory, and the dark made me afraid,
My dumb lips tried to form a wordless prayer,
I wandered, stumbling blindly as I prayed,
When through the gloom the Mount of Calvary
Loomed dark, and there my Lord nailed to the Tree.

II.

I found myself beside those bleeding feet
That brought to earth the messenger of peace,
My tears fell fast as rain, they could not cease,
Though Thy dear mercies are so blest and sweet,
Though Thy pure sacrifice was so complete
That it shall every soul from sin release,
And yield such fruit, such full and rich increase,
That all must follow when those wounds entreat.

At last, at last, yea, every eye shall see
That dual vision of God's perfect love,
Supreme surrender, glorified above;
He came to hang for us upon the Tree,
He came to feed us with the fruit thereof,
His conquering love must set the nations free!

III.

Draw me, dear Christ, by those sweet wounds that
Only beside Thy feet can I find rest,   [bleed,
My heart with sorrow and with guilt oppressed,
Aches with a knowledge of sore human need,
To clothe the naked and the hungry feed;
Could the poor wounds with oil and wine be dressed,
The little ones entreated and caressed,
The barren vineyards planted with Thy seed,
We might again see Thee transfigured here;
Strengthen us, Lord, to bring Thy harvest in,
Strengthen my hands and purge my soul from sin,
Teach me to succour weak ones when they fear,
Oh! teach me how I may one sad soul win
To Thy sweet comfort, Lord, to feel Thee near.

DAYBREAK.

"Thou makest the outgoings of the morning and evening to praise thee."—PSALM lxv. 8.

'Neath my window in the morning
    Little birds do sing :
When the sun the sky adorning
    Pearls and gold doth bring.

Eastern sky now filled with splendour,
    Bars of pearl and gold :
Songs of birds serene and tender,
    Daylight doth unfold.

And my heart walks in green meadows
    Where the daisies spring,
And I dream of cooling shadows,
    Brooks low murmuring.

Dream of all the pleasant places
    Where my feet have strayed,
Of innumerable graces
    Shewn me whilst I prayed.

If the sky and birds adore Thee,
   Making morning glad,
How shall I arise before Thee
   With my visage sad?

Let me but behold Thy beauty
   O my gracious Lord,
Every trial, every duty
   Melt to sweet accord.

While all nature sings Thy praises,
   High with rapturous thrill,
One low prayer my spirit raises
   Lord to do Thy Will.

The Virgin Mother
AND
The Vision of The Bride.

"And when they wanted wine, the mother of Jesus saith unto Him, They have no wine."—St. John ii. 3.

"Hail, Mary, full of grace, the Lord is with thee, blessed art thou among women, and blessed is the fruit of thy womb, Jesus!"

"Come hither, and I will shew thee the bride, the Lamb's wife.
"And he carried me away in the spirit to a great and high mountain, and shewed me that great city, the holy Jerusalem, descending out of Heaven from God.
"Having the glory of God: and her light was like unto a stone most precious, even like a jasper stone, clear as crystal."
Rev. xxi. 9, 10, 11.

"They have no wine," the Mother said
To Him who was the fountain head,
   Of wine the great joy giver;
"They have no wine;" the vessels fill
With water, and the Royal Will
   Made wine flow like a river.

"They have no wine," the Mother prays,
E'en now when tearful voices raise
   Their tones of sad repenting.
O blessed Mother-prayers, prevail
To bring forth wine that shall avail
   To heal past all relenting.

O Thou who art the very vine
From which flows forth the living wine,
   Strengthen our feeble praying;
Sweet Mother Mary, near us stand,
The people faint make swift demand,
   Our need brooks no delaying.

Lo! how the fig-tree languisheth,
"My very roots are parched" it saith;
   The pomegranate is failing;
The palm-tree and the apple-tree
Are perishing for lack of Thee,
   For Thee the land bewailing.

Mother, all joy is withered
From men, let tender words be said
   To call down marriage blessing,
Speak to thy Son but once again,
Bring joy unto the sons of men,
   Yea, rapture past expressing.

Thou blessed Mother of our Lord
Who gav'st to man the Incarnate word,
   In meekness God receiving;
Teach us by thy true lowliness
His Name in pureness to confess,
   Immanuel believing.

When Wisdom formed Him in thy womb,
Thy God who burst the stony tomb
   Ascending into Heaven;
Obedient to the Father's Will,
In lowliness thou did'st fulfil
   The word through ages given.

O Mother! type of womanhood,
Hidden in God, yet understood
   By thee the Lord's handmaiden,
Blessed art thou who gavest birth
To Jesus, Lord of the whole earth,
   The Man with sorrows laden.

Blessed art thou who did'st not quail,
But meekly with thy flesh did'st veil
   The Lamb, slain from foundation,
The sacrifice ordained above
To fit man for God's perfect love,
   Fruit of the chosen nation.

Thou blessed Virgin Mother mild
Who nurturedst at thy breast the Child
   For which the earth is groaning;
Breathe words of wisdom in our ear,
That hungering, thirsting hearts may hear,
   And cease their restless moaning.

"There is no wine"—the Mother's cry;
The virgins weep, and wail, and sigh,
   For their sweet Lord's appearing;
Then Israel don thy bridal dress,
He will not leave you comfortless,
   Among the nations fearing.

The water springs, that long have dried,
Shall burst forth fresh on every side;
   Thy trees with blossoms laden
Shall promise fruit; thy sons come forth,
Gathered from east, west, south and north;
   Strong youth and tender maiden.

The pasture that the fire devoured,
With herbage green springs at His word;
   The barren wildernesses
With bubbling fountains are sustained;
The flocks and herds are now regained,
   Healed of their sad distresses.

Bring offerings of drink and meat,
Bring offerings of incense sweet,
   Long from the House withholden;
Bring gifts of joy and gifts of praise,
As in the long forgotten days;
   The harvest shall be golden.

Waste not the corn, bring in the oil,
The new wine made with holy toil,
   With thrift we shall have plenty;
Fear not, O little band! though few,
The Arm Almighty strengthens you,
   And one shall be as twenty.

Proclaim the tidings glad, again,
Of " Peace on earth, good-will to men,"
   Tell aching hearts the story;
My feet upon the hills have been,
Mine eyes as from afar have seen
   His Israel crowned with glory.

Mine eyes have seen the Sun arise—
The long sad night looked with surprise
   Upon His beams of healing;
Soon that bright vision shall expand
Till every eye and ear and hand
   Shall feel the Lord's revealing.

The silver and the gold downtrod,
We then shall lift in gifts to God;
   Thy people shall be willing;
Come, Lord, with crown upon Thy head,
With hands for sacrifice outspread,
   Those hands the people filling.

Mary! among all women blest,
O golden rose! whom God hath dressed
   In robes of virgin brightness—
O garden sweet, where dwelt our Lord;
O Judah's maid by hearts adored,
   Surround us by thy whiteness.

Clothe now the Bride to meet thy Son,
Put her white robes of linen on,
   Smelling of all chief spices;
" With rows of jewels, chains of gold,
Lo! thou art fair, my Love, behold
   Thy beauty me entices."

I have found favour in his eyes;
My loved one spake, and said "Arise,
   My fair one, flowers are springing,
The Winter days are overpast,
And Spring-time sweet is come at last;
   List to the birds' low singing."

" How fragrant is the tender vine
With grapes that promise new-made wine;
   With buds the fig-tree swelling."
" Arise, my Love! my fair one, come,
Of cedar beams is built our home—
   Fir rafters bind our dwelling."

" In thy green garden blooms the rose,
And lilies there their leaves unclose,
   When soft south wind is blowing."
" Pomegranates in the orchard swell,
And pleasant fruits my Love likes well,
   By living waters growing."

In secret places of the stairs,
High up—where scarce the eagle dares
   To build—in fast recesses;
'Mid clefts of rock, there Love invites
My soul to dwell on those pure heights
   Where Nature God expresses.

Shine forth, O beauteous face appear!
Thy voice of music let me hear,
   Its sweetness me entrances;
And on the valleys low descend,
Making them green—and deign to lend
   Thy grace unto the dances.

Fresh springs of joy are found in Thee,
Tabors, and pipes, and minstrelsy,
   And ecstacy of motion;
Who made the birds' swift-wingèd grace;
The courser—fleet to run his race;
   The finny tribes of ocean.

From Thee all human joy doth spring—
The insect world, on gauzy wing,
   Quivers with exultation—
And shall not man, as happy, find
His wealth of joy in one great mind
   That formed the whole creation?

There is no joy but what He gives,
Supremest joy within Him lives,
   Yea, joy beyond comparing;
Reject Him and we suffer loss,
Nailing his love upon the cross;
   Such grief must God be sharing?

Yea, such His love that He must share
The burden that we cannot bear,
   The curse that follows sinning;
Yea, such His love, He waits to win
The souls that cleave unto their sin,
   Our free will He is winning.

Freedom He gave unto our race,
Nor will withdraw that heavenly grace,
   But by our own reception,
The "perfect law of liberty"
Upon our hearts engraved must be,
   O gift beyond conception!

Fair Bride, redeemed by God's great word,
Rent Kingdom now receive thy Lord,
   Lost Israel surrender;
Thy Ruler hath come unto thee,
And from thy sins hath set thee free,
   Behold the Bridegroom tender.

Crowned with the crown of Solomon,
The dual kingdom joined in one,
   The broken vow re-plighted;
Immanuel, rule in righteousness,
In Thee all woes shall find redress,
   Thou Man and God united!

Peter, The Rock.

"If I wash thee not, thou hast no part with me."—
St. John xiii. 8.

"Dost Thou wash me, O Master?"
　　Said Peter to his Lord;
"Dost Thou wash me, Christ Jesus?"
　　Said one who drew the sword;
"To wash my feet Thou shalt not kneel,
Said Peter, filled with righteous zeal.

"And if I do not wash thee,
　　In Me thou hast no part"
The Master said, "nor can'st thou know
　　The love within My heart;
Except I wash thee white as snow
Thou can'st not follow where I go.

"Ye must be clean to enter
　　The dens of foul disease
And take no hurt; ye must be clean
　　To speak the fair word 'Peace:'
Can ye bear witness of the light
Until its cleansing make you white?"

"Then wash my feet, O Master,
   And wash my hands and head"
Said Peter, loving his fair Lord;
   But Jesus answered—
"To wash thy hands there is no need,
Thy feet have made thee clean indeed.

"I wash thy humblest members,
   That ye may do the same
Unto the lowliest of the earth,
   Yea, wash them in My name,
As unto Me ye shall do it,
And cleanse the body every whit.

"Thus, following the commandment
   I now give unto you—
That ye should love each other;
   This, My commandment new,
That ye must follow, every one—
Do unto all as I have done.

"Then shall My Church be cleansèd,
   Then shall My Bride be fair;
Put on her spotless raiment,
   And bind her radiant hair;
My righteousness that in her lives
The garments of salvation gives.

" Like an army strong with banners,
   Like moon she shall shine forth,
The little ones shall to her cling,
   The great shall feel her worth ;
For God doth compass her around,
And in her walls shall joy be found."

The Church that erst was founded
   On Peter's own belief,
In Jesus Christ come in the flesh,
   Gained one of sinners chief,
And saints and martyrs gladly died,
Giving their lives for Christ's fair Bride.

And we must live to dress her
   In garments fair as moon ;
O lovely Bride put on thy robes,
   Thy Bridegroom cometh soon ;
Clothe thee with linen pure and fine,
To meet His Majesty Divine.

The Vision of Holy Waters.—Ezekiel xlvii.

By Shallow Streams.

By shallow streams I watched the waters play,
Clear gleam the pebbles there, and golden brown
The dead leaves lie ; the sunbeams glinting down
Through shade of trees above, make the glad way
Of waters bright, through the long sunny day;
The skies smile clear : who dreams that they can
    frown ?
Or that these waters speed to yon dark town,
Where tired hands toil till hearts forget to pray ?
Only the beauty and the joy I knew
Of summer peace, for, Oh ! my heart was blest ;
Separate from sin as far as east from west,
Unconscious of the death from which I drew
My blissful life—of death that was my due—
I only dreamed of Love, and knew God's rest.

"Waters up to the knees."
"Waters up to the loins."

My tender Father loved me while I smiled,
His gracious pity drew my heart more near
With childlike faith, I came with childlike fear,
Lisping His praises like a weanèd child;
Seeking the face of Love, whose aspect mild,
Beamed full of joy, whose voice, in tones most clear,
Made sweetest music to my waiting ear.
Onward the waters sped in streams more wild,
The deepening river, rushing as it came,
Bore me along, and as it eastward sped,
Darkness closed round, the cold hands of the dead
Clasped mine, hoarse voices called me by my name;
Some cried for comfort, some spoke words of blame;
I sought to strengthen, but fell there instead.

Waters to Swim in.

Dead with my dead! and with the sinful slain;
A broken and a contrite heart is mine;
No longer conscious of the love divine
That bore me in its arms as babe is lain
On mother's breast; my way no longer plain,
My fainting soul thirsts for the living wine,
For living bread my heart doth now repine;
I, hungering, cry, let me not call in vain;
Strength for the weary—where shall it be found
By me whom weariness hath caused to faint?
How shall I bind and heal another's wound
With wine and oil who am not free from taint?
How shall I blow my trump with certain sound
Poor sinner called to do the work of saint?

By Living Trees.

1.

Morning by morning Thou awakenest me,
With listening ear I mute before Thee stand,
Held firm in life by Thine all-strengthening hand,
Learning the truth that shall at last make free,
Sealed unto death to know Thy liberty;
Set in the limits of my narrow land,
Yet gazing upward on the starry band;
Knowing my seed countless as stars shall be.
Though I be slain, my own Redeemer lives;
Though I be dead, my flesh again shall rise;
His word of promise full assurance gives,
That cannot fail e'en though He rend the skies.
Father Almighty, under Thy broad wing
My heart shall rest in peace, my soul shall sing.

II.

The streams roll on to sweeten that dead past,
Made bitter by the ceaseless hidden flow
Of countless tears, by hearts' unuttered woe;
The dead-sea fruits—a mass of guilt I cast
Into the sea where sinks the burden vast;
Roll, living waters, cleanse that overthrow;
Lo! my Creator, faithful, I shall know,
Able to save and willing to the last.
Great is my need, Thy bounty shall supply;
Red is my sin, Thy blood shall make me white;
Death is my due, and yet with Thee I die.
Dark is my soul, behold the stars of night;
Waiting on Thee, swift wing bear me on high;
In shades of death I walk, Thy way grows bright.

For this interpretation of "The Vision of Holy Waters" I am indebted to Mrs. BREWSTER MACPHERSON. Many of the ideas here expressed may be found in her deeply interesting volume, entitled "Gifts for Men."

THE TRIUMPH OF TIME.

" Wherefore when he cometh into the world, he saith, Sacrifice and offering thou wouldest not, but a body hast thou fitted me:

"In burnt offerings and sacrifices for sin thou hast no pleasure.

"Then said I, Lo, I come (in the volume of the book it is written of me,) to do Thy Will, O God."—HEBREWS x. 5, 6, 7.

"He that seeks to save his life shall lose it : and he that loseth his life for My sake shall find it."

To do Thy Will I come; to do Thy Will
Unto the uttermost, if I be found
Worthy to stand upon such holy ground:
Here let me stand, do Thou, Lord, my cup fill
With sweet or bitter—naught can work me ill
If Thy free grace in me doth so abound,
That feeble trump give no uncertain sound,
Blown by Thy breath it wakes with sudden thrill;
My own life lost in Thee shall I not find?
My body dead, with Thee again shall rise,
Fitted to bear the glories of the skies ;
Fitted to see with eyes not long since blind ;
Fitted to comfort now the weary mind
With law of kindness—word to make men wise.

"I kill, and I make alive; I wound, and I heal; neither is there any that can deliver out of my hand."—
DEUT. xxxii. 39.

I think that I am dead, that part of me
Is dead and buried, that I knew one day
Closed in the grave and hidden quite away:
And yet that death shall no corruption see;
My spirit lives and moves in joy most free,
Yea, draws its wings from that poor silent clay;
While those still lips have now no word to say,
Another life moves on in ecstacy.
Calm in the grave one life lies cold and still;
Free in the sky another being moves;
O death in life that doth our prayers fulfil!
O life in death for every heart that loves!
O will that yieldeth to another's will—
Descending fire the sacrifice approves.

The Holy Heart.

I charge the stars to tell thee
   The words I may not speak;
I bid the flowers compel thee
   The pleasant way to seek.

I woo the winds to bind thee,
   I call the birds to sing;
The wood-doves coo to find thee,
   And home their captive bring.

I bid the red-rose blossom;
   I bid the ring-dove coo,
And carry in her bosom,
   Some dream of me to you.

For still my poor heart craveth
   To give some word or sign;
Oh! hear the word that saveth
   My love that still art mine.

Though in the grave I'm lying,
   May not my dumb heart cry?
God hear my lonely sighing,
   Make swift and sure reply.

I trust Thee though Thou slay me;
   Thy hand can wound and heal;
Thy comforting shall stay me,
   Thy precious blood shall seal.

And low beside Thine altar
   I lay my hopes and fears,
With hand that doth not falter,
   My sacrifice of tears.

My grain sown now with weeping,
   At cost of bitter pain,
With joy I shall be reaping,
   And bring my sheaves again.

My treasured hopes and dearest,
   My God, to Thee I bring;
My fondest loves and nearest,
   Here at Thy feet I fling.

My heart that still is beating
 With sacred human love,
With every throb repeating
 The height and depth thereof.

Take all its deep devotion;
 Take all its stifled cries;
Its pangs of swift emotion—
 The flame that speaks and dies.

Here safe to thine own keeping
 My heart, my life, I bring;
Still Thou its ceaseless weeping,
 And make it laugh and sing.

Bind it with sorrow broken,
 Restore what sin hath slain;
The word that shall be spoken,
 Can call to life again.

O comforting Bread sustain me;
 O strengthening Wine inspire;
Though mine own sin hath slain me,
 Consume the gift with fire.

For all I have is given—
   A broken contrite heart;
And if asunder riven,
   In Thee it has no part.

Then cleanse my sacred treasure,
   Make it as one unstained;
In death thou hast no pleasure,
   But in a heart regained.

There build a Temple lowly
   Where Holy Dove may brood,
And in that place most holy
   Feed me with living food.

There Father, Son, and Spirit,
   In unity shall reign,
The blessed meek inherit
   The earth redeemed from pain.

O, hear me Holy Father!
   O, hear me Blessed Son!
O, hear me Sacred Spirit!
   Eternal Three in One.

The Scapegoat. Lev. xvi.

Bound to the altar, I,
 Made meet to die;
Thou sent to wander free
 Over earth's rocky places;
Poor heart, dost think of me,
 Finding lost traces
Of ways we walked together
In cloudy, windy weather?
 Poor heart, so far from me,
 Lonely and free.

Alas! poor heart, I pray
For thee by night and day;
My hands and feet are bound,
My sad lips make no sound,
 And yet God hears me say
 My prayer for thee alway:
" God keep thy wandering feet,
 God keep thy heart;
God make thy life most sweet,
 Where'er thou art;
God watch between us twain
 Till life depart.

" Watch o'er my heart's desire,
   Light of mine eyes;
Make all our prayers aspire,
   Incense arise;
Guide us by cloud and fire,
   Father, All-wise."

    Though I be bound,
My spirit finds thee in far rocky places;
    I shall be found
Beside the altar, follow our lost traces
      Back to the Mercy Seat,
      Back to our God,
      There let thy lips repeat
      Words long downtrod.
Lift high the banner, lo! the Incarnate Word
Returns with flames of fire and two-edged sword.

A Farewell.

My loving words to thee,
  My body to the dust.
My soul to God who gave it me,
  In whom alone I trust.

My loving words will live
  When body shall arise,
Till then ten thousand prayers I give
  As pledges to the skies.

My shroud is long and white,
  With spice it is made sweet,
Then lay me in the summer light,
  Where shadowy branches meet.

My soul is purged from sin,
  And gladly would I go
To where the new life must begin,
  Where pain shall end I know.

My work is finished here,
  My race is almost run,
My darkened way is now made clear
  By beams of rising sun.

And heavenly light doth shine
　　Adown the angels' track;
Ah! could ye see with eyes of mine,
　　Ye would not call me back.

All faithful souls are there,
　　The many gone before,
Like incense rises ceaseless prayer
　　From true hearts that adore.

The saints and martyrs wait,
　　A glorious company,
And those who pass within the gate,
　　Their blissful splendors see.

And I among the blest
　　A humble place may crave;
My body with the dead shall rest,
　　My soul with God who gave.

I.

Though all the world frown on thee, thou hast
A love unchanging and a heart secure, [won
A love that shall through life and death endure,
And testify to deeds of valour done.
Hast thou not put the Christian's armour on
Like knight of old, because thy heart is pure?
Fight on, strong doer, thy reward is sure!
To weave thy crown the angels have begun;
And think of me as one whom thou hast set
Upon a throne in a far silent place.
Oh! not for me should thy dear eyes be wet—
Weep not, grieve not, look back a little space
Into that Paradise where first we met,
We there shall meet again, love—face to face.

II.

Let years upon this earth be long or few,
Mingled with light and shadow, sun and rain;
A good deed done outweighs a world of pain:
And we have set ourselves to work anew.
God's Word, distilled upon us as the dew,
Has filled our sinews with new life again,
Strengthened our nerves to bear the needed strain;
Strike but the chord, the sound rings brave and [true.
We work to music, singing as we go
A song of triumph that the valiant teach,
It moves majestic in its measured flow,
And is more eloquent than any speech,
And every soul must learn that song to know,
Before it can its own bright heaven reach.

The Song of the Valiant. Exodus xv.

Unto the Lord my song shall be,
   For His great triumph glorious.
The horse and rider in the sea,
   Thrown by His power victorious;
A Man of war, of sword and flame,
Jehovah is His glorious Name.

The Lord my strength, the Lord my song,
   Becomes my soul's salvation;
His kingdom will not tarry long,
   Prepare a habitation;
My father's God my God shall be,
Who saved his people from the sea.

The enemy sank down as stone,
   Who followed through the waters,
As lead a mighty host went down;
   Then sang great Israel's daughters—
" Sing to the Lord, victorious,
For His great triumph glorious."

Oh! bring Thy chosen people in
   The mountain they inherit,
And dash in pieces all their sin,
   Guide them by Thy pure Spirit,
Come with Thy glittering sword of flame,
Establish us by Thy great Name.

Hast Thou not purchased us of old?
    With precious blood hast bought us;
With wisdom, prized above all gold,
    Instructed us and taught us;
Teach us Thy song of victory,
Who saved our fathers from the sea.

Teach us a new glad song to sing,
    Of Thy new triumph glorious,
When Thou again Thy flock shalt bring
    O'er land and sea victorious,
A nation called from east and west
From north and south Thy people blest.

O God of Abraham Thy friend,
    Of Isaac, seed elected
In Jacob, chosen for this end
    To bring the King expected,
Call now the lost of Israel's race,
And gather them to their own place.

Stretch forth again Thine own right hand,
    And thunder from Thy mountain,
The sea shall surely be as sand,
    The desert as a fountain;
Oh! bid Thine exiled kingdom come,
Gather Thine outcasts to their home.

Oh! build again great Israel's house,
   Prepare the way before us,
Yea, all the mighty men arouse,
   And make them captains o'er us,
Marshal again the mighty host
Long hidden, whom the world deemed lost.

Bone to his bone shall cleave again,
   A mighty wind come rushing
To rouse the dead that had been slain,
   A fount of water gushing
Shall heal of every sad disease,
And bring the world eternal peace.

Arise! arise! Adonahy!
   Shine forth in all Thy beauty,
Let chaff before the whirlwind fly,
   Bid fire fulfil its duty.
Woman at last has called on Thee;
Arise! and set Thine Israel free.

"When once woman calls upon her God, tremble ye who desecrate her shrine. As chaff before the whirlwind, as stubble before the fire, shall ye be in the day when Adonahy shall arise in His beauty."—PARABLES OF JUDGMENT.

Six Sonnets.

I.

"If thine enemy hunger, feed him."

Mine enemy sat begging at my gates,
Anhungered, clothing torn, and visage sad;
I brought him in and gave the best I had—
Pomegranates, figs, apples and ripened dates,
And spread my bounty on great golden plates,
And looked to see mine enemy made glad;
But lo! my food to him seemed full as bad
As hunger—naught breeds good to him who hates;
Then out into the cold again he went,
And I, on my full board looked down ashamed,
And never with my food could find content,
All things seemed faulty, this and that I blamed:
Ever his hatred with each blessing blent;
My love had not yet that dark spirit tamed.

II.

"Love is the fulfilling of the law."

Then with a well-worn cloak and scanty crust
I wended forth to find my needy friend,
I came upon him just where two roads bend,
Weary and worn and travel-stained with dust,
I said, "Friend, rest awhile, yea, rest ye must,
And take my cloak, which I will gladly lend,
At your own pleasure, back to me it send,
Or keep it as a pledge of loving trust ;
Nay, more, divide with me this bit of bread.
And let us eat in friendly company."
Alas ! poor soul, never a word he said,
But his complaining—it was sad to see ;
Upon his staff he bowed his weary head,
And like a child, wept there most bitterly.

III.

"Be not overcome of evil, but overcome evil with good."

Then my sad friend back to my house I brought,
Bidding him rest, I washed his bruisèd feet;
I spread a couch for him, with spice made sweet;
I bade my chief musicians to be sought,
And charged them sing one song they had been taught,
Whose dying tones soft slumbers do entreat,
That fading strain I bade them oft repeat,
Until the veil of sleep his eyelids caught;
Refreshed and soothed by comforting healing sleep
He woke, but former woes had passed away.
"I have forgotten now why I did weep,"
Slow to himself I heard him, wondering, say,
And then he prayed that God his soul would keep;
And oh! my soul did joy to hear him pray.

IV.

"Search the Scriptures, for in them ye think ye have eternal life, but they are they which testify of Me."

I turned the pages of the Book of old,
And many a curious promise did I find;
I read to him how those who had been blind
Were made to see; how bodies dead and cold
Were made to rise; my spirit grew more bold,
I read how those possessed of devil-kind
Had been released—restored to wholesome mind;
And yet the wondrous tale was not half told:
I spoke of fountains found in desert sands;
Of angels who had walked and talked with men;
Of Israel, strengthened by upholding hands;
Of one man fighting with the power of ten;
And how the might of faith e'en death withstands,
Shutting the mouths of lions in their den.

V.

He listened, ever wondering as I spake,
And turned to me his sad beseeching eyes;
I taught to him the law that makes men wise;
I told him of One, dying for his sake:
Hearing those words his trembling soul did quake,
And all his speech did melt into great sighs.
As the shot bird quivers before it dies,
So quivered he as though his heart would break;
It was as if a mirror to his sight
Had suddenly revealed the depths below,
His darkened soul he saw made clean and white
By sacrifice supreme; he learned to know
The love, no love of man can ere requite,
And at that sight he wept, but not for woe.

VI.

And bending o'er us too the angels wept
Great tears of joy, that fell like freshening rain,
And then they sang a low enraptured strain,—
O'er golden harp strings their white fingers swept,
While lambent flames about them glowed and
 leapt;
And lengthening chords sang out like joy through
 pain,
" A soul redeemed," they cried, " brought home
 again
Into the fold, this feast day shall be kept
With songs of prayer and praise to One on high,
Who did descend to be of men the King;
From rainbow-circled throne within the sky
He comes again, let songs of triumph ring,
Let songs of rapture like the eagle fly,
And prayer's sweet incense to His altar bring."

VALEDICTION.

I.

Is my tale told and is my singing ended?
    Nay while heart beats my tale cannot be told;
True love loves on, its smiles and tears are blended
    Through all our life; its chequered lights of gold
Shine through the years into the dim beyond;
O tender hearts love on, growing more fond.

II.

When was the spider ever tired of weaving
    Her netted mesh? does she not love to spin?
Toil is her pleasure, in her fate believing,
    If rude hands break her web she doth begin
Another house, her threads drawn swift around,
A skilful plan, with measure, shape, and bound.

III.

Where is my home? where is my habitation?
    In house of many mansions shall I rest?
There have I builded on a sure foundation?
    There have I formed a little bird-like nest?
There have good deeds counted as treasure gained,
Laid up until my crown shall be attained?

IV.

My heart is there among those hidden treasures,
    My life of service here I gladly meet,
In toil and care renouncing earthly pleasures,
    Only to find eternal joys more sweet;
O rest! sweet rest! that comes with labour done;
O victor's crown after the battle won!

V.

To wrest bright virtue out of strong temptation:
    To bring forth honey from the lion's mouth:
To bind the flesh—to see the soul's salvation:
    To find wells springing in the desert's drought—
This is to know the mercy of our God,
To find our comfort in His staff and rod.

VI.

We are not vanquished, who in our strong crying
    Can bless the hand that cleanses with its scourge;
We are not vanquished in our martyr-dying,
    If songs of joy ring louder than the dirge;
We are not vanquished even while we weep,—
In anguish deep shall answer unto deep.

VII.

Fight on, brave hearts, fight out the world's old [battle,
   Eternal truth against infernal lies ;
Storm at the gates of death till thunders rattle ;
   Evil, resisted, swift before us flies !
Dash down the offspring of your darling sins,
With sword in hand the life of truth begins.

VIII.

With sword in hand the knight sees death before [him ;
   A thousand deaths rather than virtue yield,—
The body dead, angels wrap virtues o'er him ;
   The martyr with his blood his faith hath sealed,
But soon in Love's bright bower his eyes shall ope,
There shall he wake, guarded by Faith and Hope.

IX.

Oh ! many deaths we die while young life passes—
   Death of our hopes, death of our fond desires—
They wither as the flowers, and ferns, and grasses ;
   Ephemeral life in higher life expires ;
The chemist but transmutes—nothing is lost ;
Though gold of wisdom gained at sorrow's cost.

X.

Who builds the Temple of Eternal Beauty,
   With colours fair, inlaid with precious stones,
Lays down his life before the feet of duty,
   And cares not where shall rest his weary bones;
To seek and find that kingdom of great worth,
With scrip and staff content he fares him forth.

XI.

He feels not pain, he feels not body's fasting,
   His joyful spirit heavenly visions sees,
Enamoured is he of the everlasting,
   And worshipful he bends upon his knees,
On noble deeds his mind is fixed intent,
In frequent prayer his head and body bent.

XII.

And glad is he to render service lowly
   Unto some humble creature weak and old;
A child to him speaks of the Master holy,
   A lamb brings pictures of the Shepherd's fold,
And sacredness in human life is found,
Because the Father's love doth so abound.

XIII.

A pilgrim on the earth is he, and stranger,
   And yet he knows his Lord, the King of men,
He has no fear of death nor mortal danger,
   But, oh! he has a godly fear of sin;
Knowing the deadly peril to his soul,
He conquers sin at any cost or dole.

XIV.

Christ's poverty he shares, and poor in spirit
   He walks the earth, unknown by his own kind,
On earth his meekness must at length inherit,
   He lives unseen of eyes by sin made blind,
"Let all things die, so Jesus Christ be won,"
With that great prayer he girds his armour on.

XV.

To share his Master's cross, that is his glory,
   To die with Christ that he may learn to live,
To tell to all mankind the blessed story,
   And to the needy food and clothing give—
These are the hopes on which his heart is set,
And on this ground the tempter must be met.

XVI.

The lying tempter that with vain seduction
    Seeks to invest with a delusive worth
The lies that are his false brain's own production,
    A monstrous progeny of bastard birth;
And yet with specious grace they seem alive,
And for a little time do move and thrive.

XVII.

Yet woe betide the youth who at their bidding
    Seeks rest and ease in some fair green retreat;
Seize quick the sword, with sturdy blows be ridding
    The earth of them and of their foul deceit,
Dash on the stones the Babylonish brood,
The enemies of all things pure and good.

XVIII.

Take Faith, the power by which the world was
    builded,
    The motor that hath mountains great removed;
Take Hope, that many a valiant heart hath
    shielded;
    And Charity, O sweet and best beloved!
Let but these graces teach and fill thine heart,
And Satan's troop of lies must soon depart.

XIX.

Fair mistress Pride, with subtle self-deceiving,
   Tells us that we are innocent and good,
" Injured by others though past all believing "
   She whispers, feeding us with fatal food;
And Envy stirs the embers of dislike;
And Anger bids us in revenge to strike.

XX.

Idolatrous, we covet worldly blessing
   Instead of seeking out our righteous King;
Instead of meekly all our sins confessing,
   We seek repose in body's fostering;
In lust of power, of gain, of sensual feasts,
We lose our life, becoming as the beasts.

XXI.

A little sleep, we cry, a little slumber
   To rest our weary limbs, our minds repose,
Day unto day is added without number,
   Night unto night, when will the eyes unclose?
When will the watchman cry **awake! awake!**
Night is far spent, the morning **soon** will break.

XXII.

Then earth shall rise as from a gloomy pris
   Then Israel's sons and daughters shall be
A nation dead, in their great Lord re-risen,
   Cleansed from all sins, in bridal raiment dresse..
O house of Aaron, join in Judah's praise,
Our fathers' God again His power displays.

XXIII.

Levi is joined, his portion he inherits,
   Stranger no more but sheltered in the gates,
He doth not sorrow, now knowing he merits
   More than all griefs, yet joyfully he waits
The Lord's command to journey or to rest,
Obedience seems to him of all things best.

XXIV.

United now in strength his power is quelling
   The subtle forms of sin that breed disease;
The instrument of God in might dispelling
   The enemy that from his bright sword flees,
Light and perfection from his banner stream,
The Urim and the Thummim flash and gleam.

XXV.

Restore the slain, O wind of heaven fresh blowing!
    Four winds arise! breathe that these slain
      may live,
O fountain sealed, break forth again in flowing,
    Through the dry wilderness new verdure give;
Prepare the way before the coming Lord
Whose breath is sharper than a two-edged sword.

XXVI.

Turn, turn O children's hearts unto the fathers
    Lest His appearing smite us with a curse;
The faithful flock around its shepherd gathers,
    Lest dangerous wolves the little flock disperse;
In unity is strength, gather and pray,
When Shepherd calls, hear swift and swift obey.

XXVII.

He leadeth me, my Lord, by the still waters,
    In the green pastures He doth make me rest,
He calleth us by name great Israel's daughters;
    Rejoice! rejoice! in hearing ye are blest,
While we repose in dreams and slumbers deep,
He, watching us, doth slumber not nor sleep.

XXVIII.

When in the shades of death my feet do wander,
    Thy staff sustains me and Thy rod doth guide,
Upon Thy mercies sweet my heart doth ponder,
    When lo! a table spread,—on every side
Thy goodness follows me, thy love doth rush,
And in the desert living fountains gush.

XXIX.

O warrior, take thy helmet of salvation,
    Thy shield of faith to quell sin's subtle darts,
Let feet be shod with gospel's preparation
    Of peace, swift peace, to heal the aching hearts,
The armour of pure righteousness put on,
Then may'st thou fight, and victor's crown be won.

XXX.

Thy prayers that mount on high to heaven ascending
    On airy rounds a path celestial make,
Where angel visitants return descending,
    With streams of light the heavenly day doth break;
Our Father Jacob on a stone did rest,
But we now sleep on Abraham's faithful breast.

XXXI.

O Father of our race, thou now art holding
    Thine own true seed close, close in fast embrace;
Thy Father's heart is gathering and enfolding
    The little ones, while we our steps retrace
Back to the Land thy God hath given to thee,
That Holy Land redeemed, regained, made free.

XXXII.

O Father Abraham, thy blood is thrilling
    Thy children's veins again throughout the earth,
Thy faith, thy righteous faith in us instilling,
    The quickening word that gives a nation birth;
O God, in travail are Thy people born;
Rachel shall cry no more as one forlorn.

XXXIII.

Oh! happy, blessed is our generation,
    A chosen people, holy from the womb;
Saved by the Lord, our Shield, a Holy Nation,—
    Re-risen now our God hath burst the tomb;
Jehovah—Tsidkenu returns to bless;
We rise in Him, The Lord, our Righteousness.

Beatific Vision.

All I am, I give,
   All I have, I bring;
Lord, in Thee I live,
   Saviour, Lover, King;
My will grown free
    In Thee
   Mounts up with eagle wing.

As the hart pants for brooks
   So faints my soul
To feel Thy gracious looks;
   Lord, make me whole;
Thy touch my clay transmutes
   To golden fire,
And all earth's dazzling fruits
   Upon the pyre
  Consume away;
Then sound the heavenly lutes,
   The harp and lyre
Struck by immortal hands
   Yield melody supreme;
  Then breaks the eternal day;
   And in a dream
Of music shine far lands,
And lo! my soul her destiny commands,
And in Elysian fields doth will to stray.

THE TRIUMPH OF TIME.

No longer bound to mean ignoble things ;
Gifted with eagle sight and eagle wings,
Higher and higher speeds its circling flight
Beyond the clouds, beyond the gloom of night,
To where the starry one dwells on His Throne :
Ethereal splendor viewed by love alone,
Whiter than snow where sunlight clear doth rest,
Purer than down upon the dove's white breast,
Brighter than seven-fold brightness of the sun,
Softer than moon when clouds her veil put on ;
There spreads the crystal sea of molten gold,
There rainbows flash their colours manifold,
There rapturous strains of love throb out and ring
Upon the trembling air, there angels sing
Of joys that saints in Paradise have found,
And incense rises while those notes resound
In clouds of fragrant smoke saints' prayers ascend,
And with the joyful song of angels blend.
Vision of love ! vision of endless peace !
Be with me when my pilgrimage shall cease,
Be with me when my life on earth is done,
When billows all are past and victory won.

FINIS.

CONTENTS.

ORDER.		PAGE.
1	Prologue	5

PART I.
In Absence.

2	Song—" Dim forms half seen through tears " .	10
3	Why did we Part?	11
4	When I am Dead	12
5	Sea Waves	15
6	Aspiration	17
7	Song—" Unto Thee, my God, unto Thee " .	18
8	Sonnet—" That where Thou art, Thy chosen ones may be ".	19
9	Sweeter than Honey	20
10	Waters in the Desert	21
11	I gave thee Jewels	22
12	Nocturne	23
13	The Wind Harp	26
14	The Song of the Wind	27
15	Andromeda	28
16	World Weary . . . , . . .	29
17	The Lost Sheep	30

INTERLUDE—*The Tenor Voice.*

ORDER.		PAGE.
18	Wingèd Sleep	37

PART I. CONTINUED.

19	Avenged	41
20	Relenting	42
21	Yearning	43
22	Light in Darkness	44
23	Strong as Death	45
24	Dreams of the Night. No. I.	46
25	Joy in Sorrow	47
26	Twilight Mists	49
27	Dreams of the Night. No. II.	50
28	Hymn of Praise	51
29	Pre-Vision	53
30	Wrestling	55
31	Tyre	56
32	Weary	59
33	The Comforter	60
34	The Song of the Dove	61
35	Dead Desire	65

PART II.

The Word Restored.

36	Hymeneal Hymn	71
37	Recompense	78
38	The Land of Silence	79
39	Sonnet—"O my Belovèd, hide and rest in me"	82
40	Seek and ye shall find	83

CONTENTS.   225

PART III.
Judgments.

ORDER.		PAGE.
41	Follow after Love . . .	87
42	The Sacrificial Doves. No. I. . .	89
43	Interlude	91
44	The Sacrificial Doves. No. II. . . .	92
45	Song—" By Bread alone we do not live " .	94
46	Saved as by Fire	95
47	Song—" Flesh of thy flesh I am " . . .	97
48	Thou Knowest	99
49	Song—" Like an avalanche, my Love runs fast "	103
50	Christian Marriage	105
51	Mystical Death	108
52	" The strange, sad charm of Death " . . .	110
53	A Night of Roses	112
54	Song—"Across the Sea"	113
55	The Wingèd Harp	114
56	Song—" Where Lilies blow, my Love doth feed "	114
57	Sonnet—" Henceforth I will believe that thou dost love "	115
58	Song—" What hast thou given to me " . .	116
59	Chorus—" Wingèd heart, wingèd lyre " . .	117

PART III.
Building The House

60	The Name	121
61	Building the House	122
62	The City Lieth Four Square	129

INTERLUDE.—*Confession and Absolution.*

63	Sonnet—" I have renounced Love's ways " . .	131
64	Sonnet—" O Love, I bartered all, nor counted cost	132

P

ORDER.		PAGE.
65	Sonnet—"And thus I tread a path of loneliness"	132
66	Sonnet—"And yet from that dead waste there may arise"	133

THE THREAD RESUMED.

67	Song—"O sweet Oblivion"	137
68	When Beauty Fades	137
69	Sonnet—"So I be fair to thee"	138
70	Sonnet—"Yea, love me so before my roses fade"	138
71	When Roses Bloom.	139
72	The Sacrament . . . . . , .	140
73	The Meeting	140
74	Sonnet—"Yea, in Love's sacred and most hidden Bower"	141
75	Sonnet—"Though night be dark, the long watch I will keep"	142
76	Song—"O my dear Soul"	142
77	Song—"Where shall my bark drift" . .	143
78	Within and Without	144
79	The Star-Fish	145
80	Sonnet—"Better the Silence"	148
81	The Hidden Bower	149
82	Song—"Sometimes I almost faint to think" .	154
83	Autumn Song . , ...	155
84	Song—"Yea, those who tread the desert's track	159
85	At Communion	159
86	Sonnet—"I will be calm, I will not speak nor sigh"	160
87	Sonnet—"Too soon? ah! no, since led by Love's own hand	161
88	Willow Song	162
89	Song—"I have an armèd knight" . . .	163
90	Song—"A bonnie bird came flying" . . .	164

ORDER.		PAGE.
91	The Angel of Our Love	165
92	The Dual Vision—Three Sonnets.	166
93	Daybreak	168
94	The Virgin Mother and the Vision of the Bride	170
95	Peter, The Rock	179
96	By Shallow Streams.	182
97	"Waters up to the knees." "Waters up to the loins."	183
98	Waters to Swim in	184
99	By Living Trees	185
100	Sonnet—"The streams roll on to sweeten that dead past"	186
101	Sonnet—"To do Thy Will I come; to do Thy Will"	187
102	Sonnet—"I think that I am dead"	188
103	The Holy Heart	189
104	The Scapegoat	193
105	A Farewell	195
106	Sonnet—"Though all the world frown on thee"	197
107	Sonnet—"Let years upon this earth be long or few"	198
108	The Song of the Valiant	199

SIX SONNETS.

"If thine enemy hunger feed him."

109	I. "Mine enemy sat begging at my gates"	202
110	II. "Then with a well-worn cloak and scanty crust"	203
111	III. "Then my sad friend back to my house I brought	204
112	IV. "I turned the pages of the Book of old"	205
113	V. "He listened, ever wondering as I spake"	206
114	VI. "And bending o'er us too the angels wept"	207
115	Valediction	208
116	Beatific Vision	219

FARQUHARSON ROBERTS & PHILLIPS,
PRINTERS,
13, HUGGIN LANE, QUEEN VICTORIA STREET, LONDON, E.C.

Fscp. 8vo., Cloth.

THE
TRIUMPH OF LOVE.

A

Mystical Poem

IN SONGS, SONNETS AND VERSE,

BY

ELLA DIETZ.

LONDON:
E. W. ALLEN, 4, AVE MARIÁ LANE.
MDCCCLXXVII.

THE ENGLISH PRESS.

THE EXAMINER.

There is no ordinary depth and tenderness of feeling in these poems. They have a curious resemblance in sentiment to the mystical poetry of the seventeenth century. Such a song as the following might have been written by a female George Herbert :—

> O touch me not, unless thy soul
>   Can claim my soul as thine ;
> Give me no earthly flowers that fade,
>   No love, but love divine :
> For I gave thee immortal flowers,
> That bloomed serene in heavenly bowers.
>
> Look not with favour on my face,
>   Nor answer my caress,
> Unless my soul have first found grace
>   Within thy sight ; express
> Only the truth, though it should be
> Cold as the ice on northern sea.
>
> O never speak of love to me,
>   Unless thy heart can feel
> That in the face of Deity
>   Thou wouldst that love reveal :
> For God is love, and His bright law
> Should find our hearts without one flaw.

VICTORIA MAGAZINE.

From this book it is scarcely possible to make an extract ; it must be read in its entirety. Until we came to the last page the book never left our hand. Every line betrays intense earnestness ; and mystical as it may be, human love and anguish throb and surge throughout, until the final chorus is reached :—

> Out of each heart there went a flame,
> And rose till it came to the Great White Throne,
> And there the two were made as one,
> And as those flames ascend, aspire,
> God accepteth the gift of fire,
> And giveth instead His own bright Name.

THE CIVILIAN.

As an actress and reader of no mean ability, the authoress of this work has for some years past been before the London public. Nor is this, we believe, her first essay in Authorship, for, unless we are greatly mistaken, we have seen her name subscribed to several gracefully-written scraps of verse which have appeared from time to time in the periodical press. The present work is of a more ambitious character than any of these, but it is of an equal, indeed of a higher order of excellence. The depth of feeling, elegance of fancy, and purity of diction, which lend so great a charm to her slighter effusions, are present also here ; and with them we note an occasional sublimity of thought, a breadth and loftiness of conception, which mark her possession of powers far beyond those of the mere writer of verse. The general character of the poem reminds one somewhat of "In Memoriam," and indeed the influence of Tennyson is visible in nearly every page. The following lines, to give an example, might well pass as the composition of the Poet Laureate, and are certainly not unworthy of his pen :—

> I would that I could marry my sweet thought
> To words that should convey the soul of sense ;
> Clothe it with language pure, sublime, intense,
> And wondrous rhythm with such meaning fraught
> That every ear might hear, and by it taught
> Pierce through these Babel clouds so thick and dense,
> That hide us each from each—

The authoress does not fall far short of her aspiration, for her poem is full of beautiful thoughts, expressed in language as powerful as it is graceful. The work deserves to be read.

PUBLIC OPINION.

This is a very carefully-written volume of verse, of a pathetic nature, and bearing the marks of refinement and delicacy. The authoress has evidently a great power of versification.

Herrick has shown that an almost Catulline fancy

in the weaving of love-poetry is not incompatible with a higher appreciation of the beauties of a purer style. He managed by his writing to bridge over the chasm between the nature-worshipping of sense and the ideas of the inner man. Miss Dietz has well followed in the path which Herrick has indicated, and her verse is redolent of the prairie flower.

THE GRAPHIC.

Is by no means wanting in metrical ability, or in thoughtfulness, though the author may occasionally appear to sound unfathomable depths. The gist of the whole seems to be the apotheosis of faithful love, the human leading up to the divine; and the best passages are those entitled " Sursum Corda," " Day Song," " Night," and " Love's Gifts."

THE PUBLISHER'S CIRCULAR.

It might almost be called a lady's *In Memoriam*, penetrated by an intensely devout frame of mind, and clad in words of fitting solemnity and beauty.

SUNDAY TIMES.

Few volumes of modern poetry deserve a warmer welcome than *The Triumph of Love* of Miss Ella Dietz. Tender, thoughtful, and womanly throughout, it rises at points into absolute inspiration, and it has every variety of charm that cultivation, fervent aspiration, and poetic perception can bestow. Its attractions for the reader will be increased when he knows that the author is an artist who has won herself position upon the stage. A work must, of course, stand upon its own merits and be judged apart from all personal claim of the author. When, however, tested by the most rigid standard, it wins admiration, the fact that the author has claims of another class cannot fail to enhance the interest it possesses. Not so accustomed, indeed, are our artists to go out of themselves and seek distinction in kindred walks that we can be otherwise than grateful when we find an instance such as this in question. We accord thus a warm reception to a book that needs no such recommendation, for the fact that its writer is one who has won our admiration by the display of other phases of her talent.

* * * * * * * *

It is involved in the very conditions under which a poem like this is written that it is impossible to give by separate extracts an idea of the sustained grace, beauty and tenderness of the whole. This, however, is the only resource left us. The reader who seeks to comprehend the relation to each other of the different portions headed by such names as "Retrospection," "Introspection," "The Reality," "The Temptation," and "The Triumph," the recurrent sweetness of the refrains or the pathos of the "Interludes" must turn to the volume.

THE ERA.

The fair writer of the poem seems to have attempted a mystical poem something after the School of Dante Rosetti's "House of Life." Her poetical talents are considerable and some of the songs in this volume are remarkably flowing and graceful; we may instance that commencing "Wake, Wake the Dawn is Breaking" and another "Starry Eyes."

THE SPIRITUALIST.

This poem is essentially a creation. It is intensely subjective; but are not all great poems more or less so—or, at all events, are not poems great *to us;* do they not take hold upon us, in proportions as they reveal the inner self of the poet, or (in this case) the poetess?

Perhaps the highest testimony that could possibly be given to the holiness of the poem is afforded in the circumstance that a clergyman of the Church of England, who is not wont to quote words at random in the pulpit, and whose congregation is one of the largest in London, selected some words from *The Triumph of Love* to conclude a sermon on Christ's sketch of His mission, as given by St. Luke in the description of His sermon in the Nazarene synagogue. The words of the poem are, in fact, little more than a paraphrase of Holy Writ at this point :—

> My spirit travaileth to give new birth
> To light; to lift and let the oppressed go free;
> Draw all their sins and sorrow unto me,
> And suffer once for all; to give them mirth
> For tears; to feed the hungry hearts; for dearth
> Plenty and riches, faith and charity.

The book must be read more than once to master its meaning ; but those who have been privileged to make one perusal will need no persuasion to induce a second.

MAURICE DAVIES.

THE PSYCHOLOGICAL REVIEW.

Every true poet, yea, every original thinker, is a mystical teacher for some stage of initiation into the hidden life, and every one by birthright has entered into one or more of its degrees. He is more immediately and widely heard who can give expression to the mystic feeling of the greater number. * * * The writer seems to have drank deeply of the well of our best Elizabethan poets ; some verses remind us of Spenser, and the unity of purpose and subject of the sonnets of those of Shakespere.

THE SUNDAY REVIEW.

As the title indicates, Love is the theme of this collection of poems, which are very musical, and often very mystical, and form not so much a continuous relation, as a series of expressions of mental phases and alternations of feeling, doubt, hope, fear, temptation, triumph. The aim of the writer is high and pure; setting forth love, filling two hearts and overflowing until it embraces all humanity and all God's visible creation; subduing self in devotion to duty; finding blessed peace amidst the woes and trials of earthly life, and resting at last in the great Centre and Source of life and love, having its fulness and completeness in God. One of two lovers, the woman, dreams that being denizens of heaven, they seek and obtain permission to descend to earth to give to the world this lesson of unselfish love, to teach mankind that thus alone can their brotherhood with Christ be made manifest and their union with God completed.

It is the woman whose mission it is to carry on this blessed work, and to make the dream a reality, showing man his divine nature, making him at one with God. A fitting corollary to the old story of Eve tempting Adam to fall; woman at last, through pure love, tramples under foot the old serpent Selfishness, brings home to man's consciousness the love which Christ died to make manifest to him, and so restores him, purified from sin, to his lost Eden.

In the working out of the theme, the most ardent sensuous love is refined and spiritualised, as the oriental mysticism of Solomon's Song is made to typify the affinity of Christ and His Church. The grand lesson inculcated is that which the best minds of all ages and of all creeds have believed and taught, universal love, charity in its highest sense, without which theological dogmas are but as dry husks, and the law of God unapprehended.

SUSSEX DAILY NEWS.

Miss Dietz is especially happy in that most difficult of all forms of composition, the sonnet; and some of the snatches of song with which, as in the Old Greek Tragedy, she marks the breaks in her poem, are perfect gems.

THE THEATRE.

It is full of poetic feeling and graceful imagery, and many of the lines will live in the memory of those who read them.

THE KENSINGTON NEWS.

We are indeed amazed at the fertility and wealth of ideas comprised in this little volume and its fragmentary contents; while the moral, contained in two lines of an ode called " Sursum Corda," must commend itself to our very highest regards :—

> 'Till we reflect God's glory here,
> We cannot pass to His bright sphere.

Next in beauty to the Sonnets are the Songs, freely interspersed through the poem, in many different metres, and often as exquisite as those in *Festus*.

THE ACADEMY.

If the book is simply an expression of human love, it is very graceful and full of poetical feeling. In their first and obvious meaning some of the sonnets are beautiful. We quote one from the early part of the book :—

> "Should we part now? O love, how can we part?
> Leave if thou wilt, thou canst not take away
> The glory and the brightness of the day.
> My soul will be with thine where'er thou art;
> Till thou canst send the red blood from thy heart
> Thou canst not banish me, though I may stay
> As silently; still shall my silence pray
> Until thy spirit feel the vital smart.
> I would not have thee suffer. O my own,
> I would not hold thee, thou shouldst still be free,
> For when thou goest I am not alone,
> Thou canst not take thyself away from me :
> But thou canst dim the brightness of the sun
> With clouds. O love! I would not have thee gone!"

www.ingramcontent.com/pod-product-compliance
Lightning Source LLC
Chambersburg PA
CBHW021815230426
43669CB00008B/760